LEADERSHIP TURNAROUND

IFIE SEKIBO, PHD

Publishing services by EVANGELISTA MEDIA & CONSULTING
publisher@evangelistamedia.com
www.evangelistamedia.com

ISBN: 978-88-6880-123-6

For Worldwide Distribution, Printed in Italy.

1 2 3 4 5 6 / 23 22 21 20

Dedication

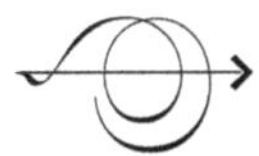

This piece of work is dedicated to all who are committed to stretching and dreaming big to bring value to our world. May God work through us to accomplish the bigger purpose of shaping and transforming lives by the work of our hands.

Acknowledgments

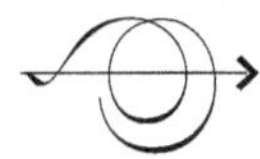

It is simply amazing how our lives are shaped and made better by the gifts of exposures, experiences and interactions. I thank everyone who in one way or the other has contributed to the success of this book. Especially my special assistant, Sunny Awoyemi, who kept pushing me to put down my thoughts for the next generation of leaders.

I appreciate most profoundly Dr Linus Okorie who made it his personal project that I do not give up; I owe more than a thank you to him. My heartfelt appreciation to Dr Tonye Ifie Sekibo for her great support and encouragement.

I thank my children, especially Gbeye, Deinma, Ibifuro, Minainyo, Soalanabo, and Tamunoemi for encouraging me in the challenging times. Dr May Ikeora is not left out of my appreciation for telling me it's possible. Bishop David Oyedepo, my spiritual father, thank you for teaching me about leadership in a special way.

My friends, Ndutimi Alaibe, Sokpiri Graham Douglas, Prof. Steve Azaiki, Dr Alex Otti, Chris Oshiafi, Fidelis Anosike and many more are not left out of my appreciative mind.

My most praise and thanks goes to Jesus Christ – my Saviour, Model and Friend.

Endorsements

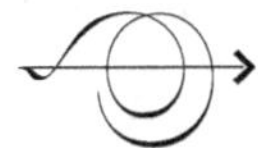

Mr Sekibo enjoys nothing more than to see people succeed with their business and personal endeavours. He understands the principle that a great leader does not merely create followers, rather they create more great leaders.

He holds dear to his heart his business dreams, goals, plans, passions and wishes. He knows that succeeding occurs only when you take action; and like an artist placing images on canvas, so do people of action move on with their dreams, ideas and aspirations. I coined the word 'Actionaire', referring to one who takes on those dreams, ideas and aspirations with courage, confidence and bravado. This book recognises that this is the secret to happiness. Exploring action develops the possibilities within your lifetime.

As part of one's efforts to reach their possibilities, there requires the manifestation of certain principles described by Mr Sekibo. These principles will assist you in the development of a quality lifestyle. Winning requires a variety of skills and principles. Winners are those who have tried and lost but did not quit or give in to the temptation of being preserved as a failure.

The day you realise that there is no such thing as failure, is the day you become a true champion. Why do I say that? I say to you there is no such thing as failure, only experiences where the outcome wasn't as you would have liked. Rather, it is a gainful exercise that will only strengthen you in the future.

Becoming a champion doesn't begin around you; it starts inside you. In your mind, is where you will begin to experience the happiness of a winner! In your mind, you will frame your future.

The Actionaire's secrets to happiness are to embrace the wisdom and art of capitalism contained in this book. Capitalism is an economic system based on the private ownership of the means of production and operation for profit. In a capitalist market economy, decision-making and investment are determined by every owner of wealth, property or production ability in financial and capital markets, whereas prices and the distortion of goods and services are mainly determined by competition in these respective goods and services markets.

You must declare that the happiest and most productive days of your life are starting now! With 86,400 seconds in your day, you must never take your mind off your mission. Why? Because some of your possibilities may be achievable within the next second of your existence.

Thank you, Ifie Sekibo, for writing a book where each page gives its readers the lessons needed to achieve their life's goals.

Dr Michael V. Roberts
JD International
Best-Selling Author of *Action Has No Season*
Businessman

Leadership Turnaround is a groundbreaking book. It is profoundly insightful and inspirational. Ifie Sekibo brings his scholarship to the subject of leadership, mindset and attitude that will determine both an individual's and a nation's place in this highly competitive world. To define your legacy and make your mark, you have to identify the vehicle of leadership as an essential pathway to success.

Through his inspiring story of recharging a once lifeless company into one of the leading exemplary institutions in Nigeria, he has modelled one of the key examples of transformational leadership that is scarce in our world. His inspiring strategies, stories and insights are told with simplicity and power. They are the timely guideposts necessary today for building and sustaining a life or business in a 21st century globally competitive environment.

This book, no doubt, will expose every discerning mind to an important work through which a personal rebranding occurs that guides you to your purpose in life. Don't play on the lower rungs of the ladder anymore. Buy this masterwork and climb, for you now have been equipped to ascend step by step to the stars. I found Ifie's thoughts in this book a profoundly instructive and inspiring read; to that end, I highly recommend it for you.

Dr George C. Fraser
Author, *Success Runs in Our Race*
President, FraserNation
Cleveland, Ohio, USA

Leadership is one subject that so many texts have been written about. Despite this fact, we can't have enough of it: the more, the merrier. So, when the author spoke to me about the book he was writing, many things came to my mind.

Looking at his background, position, exposure and experience, he is qualified to give his perspective on the subject. Although the problem of leadership is arguably one of the most important ones facing our country today, there is this tendency for many writers to oversimplify it by narrowing it down to political leadership alone. That is why one would not be surprised if an accomplished banker and entrepreneur focuses on it.

Often, we intend to forget that we are all leaders in our own rights – in our families, businesses, churches, mosques and communities. We can all make a difference where we are only if we can deliberately expand the way we perceive leadership and allow ourselves to participate in the conversation, not as passive bystanders but as active participants.

Perusing through this book, one will immediately discover that the author delivered on his promise to lead a conversation on such a very important subject matter in our polity, especially when viewed in the context of preparation for leadership in Africa. The elements of this conversation are rich, and the sources of his experience are diverse and eclectic.

Central to the leadership success of the author is the building of a brand-new Heritage Bank from the wreckages of the defunct Societe Generale Bank of Nigeria. For those who are familiar with the kind of challenges and bottlenecks that would normally accompany such feat, the author is more than a visionary adventurer.

He is a professional banker who has risen to the top echelon of his profession by foresight, courage and by treading where others dread.

In this book, you will hear a blend of voices all fused into one. You will hear a deep philosopher and a patient teacher. You will be particularly enchanted by the team-building skills of the author and will discover how division of labour contributed greatly to the transformation that has become the inspiring story behind Heritage Bank's success. Yet Ifie had the humility to insist that a good leader must 'create an idea, leave it on the dance floor and go to the balcony'.

The author, born in the oil-rich Niger Delta, undoubtedly possesses that unique quality of patriotism and inclusiveness that has become the pride of the Niger Delta story. Though an accountant by profession, a banker by calling, Ifie Sekibo's background certainly has prepared him to write this book.

I have known him for over twenty years and can attest to the distinctive resilience and industry that defines him. This naturally made his analogy of the use of crude oil and its refining process to mentoring very outstanding and in many ways similar to my own story. As I read this book, thoughts kept flashing in my mind of what my story could have been if I did not have the benefit of the refining process that good mentoring from visionary leaders can produce in diligent mentees.

As a student of leadership myself, this book has a lot to teach me, especially now that I am actively participating in our political process.

The biggest dilemma of political leadership in the African continent, especially in Nigeria, in my view, is how to create an enabling environment to provide a transition to a more sustainable, non-oil economy before the oil in our country dries up. The author lucidly shares practical experiences about how to revamp the small and medium enterprises, something he has experimented successfully with his team in the bank and which can be replicated for the benefit of others both within and beyond Nigeria.

For me, the most impactful part of this conversation is the author's emphasis on attitude to vision and wealth creation. At the end, such fertile mindset of possibilities, the tenacity to overcome challenges, the capacity for optimal thinking and the addiction to positive results, stand out as the biggest legacies that the author will leave behind if and when he decides to move on to other endeavours.

This book will greatly enrich the reader. The experience of this illustrious banker and citizen of the world comes to play in this book on leadership, entrepreneurship and human capacity building. The author has not claimed total and complete knowledge of the subject matter; therefore, the reader must take it as his personal experience not a text claiming monopoly of knowledge or expertise. I enjoyed every bit of it and wish every attentive reader, a similar experience.

Steve Azaiki, PhD, Oon
Pro-Chancellor and Chairman of Governing Council
Niger Delta University

CONTENTS

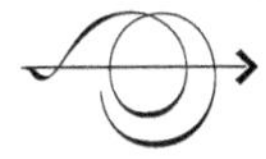

FOREWORD

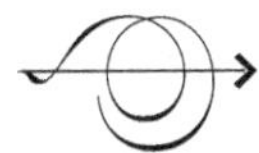

It is said that the half-life of knowledge in this age is six months. That means half of whatever you know will be obsolete in six months' time. This in itself poses as a challenge to organisations in meeting their client's or customer's expectations.

As a speaker, author and consultant to tens of thousands of companies around the world, I can tell you that most companies never grow to their full potential because of the leader's inability to keep up with the pace of knowledge in this era. The forces of capitalism are creatively destroying organisations that cannot compete favourably. This effect continues to purge leaders in different sectors, allowing the best to keep re-emerging every time. Those leaders who are not well equipped for the turn, eventually get lost in it.

Leadership Turnaround helps to analyse the turns involved in leading organisations today with so much emphasis on building the organisation for long-term success.

Dr Ifie Sekibo has carefully put together this masterpiece detailing with simplicity his journey of turning around a moribund company into a global conglomerate under the harsh economic weather of the Nigerian economy. He has redefined leadership in such a way that everyone could relate to it and use it in daily living. His journey through these years of turning around an organisation once perceived to be almost dead without hope of resurrection is phenomenal. The lessons are timeless.

Bringing vision and enterprise into one mould is one heck of a difficult task. Dr Ifie Sekibo carefully balanced the two in this book. It is often true that many leaders easily jump out in pursuit of vision of the organisation, but very few can do so in an enterprising manner. It is not enough to know what you want to achieve, you have to know how to actually achieve it and then sustain it. That is the bane of the enterprising leader.

In this journey of leadership, one must brace up to the challenges of leading. To successfully navigate this sea of obstacles, the leader must possess a certain mindset of growth that allows him to innovate continually. Dr Ifie explained how he turned around the fortunes of a moribund financial institution by first changing the mindset of the people he worked with. The leader's mindset in an organisation is key to leadership turnaround. The leader must believe in himself and the possibilities that others don't even see. In leadership, belief is a strong asset of the leader.

I believe that every young person who aspires to be a leader will benefit tremendously from this book. *Leadership Turnaround* is not just furnished with rich information to equip the youths to lead, but the book strongly advocates for one to take responsibility early in life.

This book is not just for business leaders but for political leaders as well. People are the essence of any true leadership. Dr Ifie continues to emphasise and affirm all through the pages of this book that 'without values, vision and mission become mere poetry'. As you flip through the pages of this book, I encourage you to do so with your imagination, and actively engage the thoughts of the author. The pictures and experiences of Dr Ifie Sekibo will begin to come alive to you like it did to me. This is not just another book on leadership, this is a leadership journey. Enjoy your read…

Brian Tracy
Author of *Earn What You're Really Worth*
CEO, Brian Tracy International
Bankers Hill, San Diego, California

INTRODUCTION

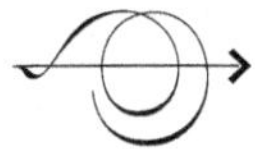

It has been both a privilege and a real pleasure for me to be asked to write this brief introduction to Ifie Sekibo's book, *Leadership Turnaround*. Thank you for giving me this honour.

My pleasure stems in part from the fact that while so many books on leadership are written by academics who have never led a flock of sheep, let alone people, Ifie's book has the hallmark of practical experience written all through it.

Ifie knows firsthand what it is like to lead the way in difficult and challenging times. He led the team to acquire the moribund Societe Generale Bank of Nigeria, which had been dead for ten years, and transformed it into a thriving and respected bank. The fascinating and instructive story behind that remarkable achievement unfolds vividly in the following pages.

To be a really good teacher of leadership to the younger generation, however, personal experience of leading others is not enough. You need also to understand the underlying and eternal principles of leadership. For it is those principles that you, the reader, will want to take away and apply in your own and probably very different field of work.

Ifie mentions more than once the importance of having the mindset of a leader. That mind includes the way you think about people, both persons in general and in particular, about the team you are called to lead. Remember always that, as John Buchan said, 'the task of leadership is not to put greatness into humanity, but to elicit it, for the greatness is already there'.

Nigeria is a great country and therefore it deserves great leaders. Thankfully, in this outstanding book, Ifie has given us the kind of thoughts, stories and examples that will inspire you to become a great leader yourself. And by that I mean a 'good leader and a leader for good'. Happy reading!

John Adair
World-Renowned Leadership Authority
Prolific Author

Chapter 1

THE VEHICLE OF LEADERSHIP – VISION

So much emphasis has been placed on vision without the accompanying leadership, or better put, attitude to drive it. Anybody can have a vision, but living it goes beyond just having it. Without the right attitude or mindset, vision can't be realised.

By way of further elucidation, I always give an illustration from the Bible. Genesis 11:1-9 tells the story of when humankind had a vision to build a tower high enough to reach the heavens. God noticed their level of commitment and also observed that they were of *one mind*. In other words, they had a common mindset. God resolved to come down and create dissension among them so that they would have different languages, or mindsets (Genesis 11:6-7). This narrative clearly illustrates that vision is a function of mindset and attitude. So we can say *attitude drives vision.*

Mindset is everything. Mindset determines the outcome of every endeavour. One can tell the end of an activity from the beginning by looking at the mindset. In the example from the Bible, God saw that the people were going to be successful because they had one mind, saying, 'Indeed the people are one and they all have one language' (Genesis 11:6a). One mind means having unity of thoughts or conclusion. So once the minds of people can be united on a common front, they become unstoppable unless a higher force is able to overcome it.

No nation or individual can achieve success without having a unified focus. America is called the United States of America (USA) because those who founded it had a oneness of thought or vision that united them. They had one mind. Today, Nigeria is the way it is because we have not been able to achieve that unity or one mindedness.

Leadership is the vehicle for achieving oneness of vision. The leader does this by motivating a group of people to believe in themselves. At times, some who have found themselves in positions of leadership get it wrong by believing that leadership is all about getting people to believe in them, the leaders. This is not only wrong, the effects are devastating as the so-called leader becomes the one eyed in a land of the blind, and chaos results from the pressure generated.

In leadership, the focus is on the people. A true leader understands the magnitude of the project and how it goes beyond the strength of one individual. In other words, the leader understands the concept of partnerships. To galvanise minds toward a goal requires an ability to understand the limitations of that mind and working toward eliminating obstacles. There is a saying that whether you think you can or can't – you are right. The mind is like a machine that churns out whatever we believe or agree is possible.

So the task of leadership is to make others see things from a particular perspective, which compels them to buy into a vision or project. A leader has the mindset of an entrepreneur and relentlessly drives the vision regardless of the resources at his or her disposal. Thomas Edison, a famous inventor, failed a thousand times in his quest to invent the incandescent light bulb. Naturally, the average Joe would have given up, but Edison didn't give up. In fact, he said that through his failures he just discovered a thousand ways that didn't work. Such is the mindset of an entrepreneur, which is so critical to leadership.

Oftentimes, people see the entrepreneur as a risk taker, when he is simply the one who forges ahead when others are reclining. A mindset is a powerful force and can be seen in the giant strides of commerce and industry. A corporation is a mindset because it requires people of like minds to come together under a unified purpose. The cold war between the USA and USSR was a mindset. Critical to a mindset is the underlying assumption(s). The task of the leader is to create a mindset, to discover these underlying assumptions, study them and influence them in a way that brings about a conviction toward the leader's intended course.

As stated, a leader has the mindset of an entrepreneur. A lot of people believe that an entrepreneur is a risk taker when he is simply the one who has resolved to push on regardless of the obstacles. So, he looks for those who have the resources and convinces them to buy into the vision. The leader builds a team by bringing like minds together and inspiring them. He builds confidence in them by helping them to redefine themselves. A leader understands the concept of synergy, which is the only way humans can achieve much more than what they can individually. A leader understands that leadership is a situational expertise.

In other words, a leader assumes different roles at different times and to different people. As a leader, you can't be the same person in every circumstance. In your house, you must become the father. In your marriage, you must become the husband. In your organisation, you become the CEO. Trying to be the same person in all circumstances and contexts exposes you to mistakes. It is through this entrepreneurial mindset of the leader and his team that big corporations are built.

In a country like Nigeria, we must deliberately enthrone a leader or leadership that via inspiration influences the mindsets of the people. Leadership is so central to vision and nation building that we need to begin to introduce leadership to the youth at an early age. As we encourage them to assume leadership positions early in life, they begin to overcome the inertia that drives them away from positive things that make not just for their good alone but for the good of all. In this vein, we must encourage the youth to be captains of the football team, we must encourage them to be patrol leaders in the Boy Scouts, we must encourage them to lead the marching band. We must create the leadership mindset in them early. We must instill in them a mindset of possibilities.

A practical example of what can be achieved with a mindset of possibilities is orchestrated in the story regarding the Societe Generale Bank of Nigeria (SGBN).

REVIVING THE DEAD

SGBN was moribund for more than ten years when we took it over. It was a dead vessel that no one believed could be resuscitated. There was nothing left of the bank that pointed toward the possibility of a resurrection. However, I had a positive mindset of possibilities that enabled me to foster the belief that the bank could rise again.

I didn't have all the requirements at my disposal then; but due to my belief, I began to build a team and partnerships around the endeavour. I had to create the mindset of the team by redefining the problem and presenting various possibilities – and by so doing, I opened their minds to a different perspective. We overcame challenges because we allowed our thoughts to transcend the obstacles we met on our way. With this mindset we gave life to a bank that was dead for more than a decade. We bought over the bank and paid back all the monies owed to customers trapped in the dead bank. We then created a new bank, now called Heritage Bank.

CREATING THE PROPER MINDSET

Organisations do not become the best by themselves but can become the best if the individuals who drive them have the necessary mindset to make it so. This is why I say *vision is nothing without the right attitude or mindset to push it to success.* You can't change a mindset without demanding it to define the problem and the easiest way to understand someone's mindset is to hear their perspective of a problem. You will become aware of their limitations, which gives you a starting point to begin influencing them positively.

It is essential in our efforts to change the mindsets of the youth to get them out of their current mindset and alter them to be the best they can become. Many are stuck in this rut and won't overcome until they are mentored out of it. We must get them to transcend their current circumstances and keep their eyes on the goals they want to achieve. We must train them to think optimally. The culture or mindset of self that is prevalent in the youth today must be changed to a mentality of us and we. For us to experience economic, political or social transformation, we must erase the self-serving notion of the word 'I' from our vocabulary and replace it with 'we'.

Behaviourally, there are two categories of mindset into which individuals can be grouped: *fixed* mindset and *growth* mindset. Those who have a fixed mindset believe that abilities are innate. Those with a growth mindset believe that skills can be acquired through investment of effort and study. So, the leader needs to discover the underlying assumptions of an individual or group's mindset, and attempt to be an influence. If a negative mindset is discovered, he tries to influence it positively.

The idea of having two mindsets may be a new concept for many, but it's so vitally important to understand this and make the decision of which concept to embrace. Some may think it's easy to toggle between the two, but it's not. For some, these mindsets have been predetermined and dominate their entire thought process. Without proper acknowledgment of where a person is, they may suffer needlessly for this lack of information. For the growth mindset, additional information is needed.

FIXED VERSUS GROWTH MINDSETS

Fixed and growth mindsets are terms coined by Carol Dweck, PhD, author of *Mindset: The New Psychology of Success*, to describe beliefs regarding personal qualities such as ability and talent. According to research, the fixed mindset tends to believe that attributes such as ability and skill are set. Maria Popova recaps Dweck's insights on fixed mindset with these words:

> A 'fixed mindset' assumes that our character, intelligence, and creative ability are static givens which we can't change in any meaningful way, and success is the affirmation of that inherent intelligence, an assessment of how those givens measure up against an equally fixed standard; striving for success and avoiding failure

at all costs become a way of maintaining the sense of being smart or skilled.[1]

Malcolm Ocean, a self-proclaimed multipotentialite and jack-of-all-trades, said while digging deeper into his knowledge of Carol Dweck's research,

> Both a growth mindset and a fixed mindset have the delightful property of being self-reinforcing. People who have growth mindset will tend to improve, which will reinforce the idea that ability is learnable. People who have fixed mindset will tend to stagnate, which will reinforce the idea that they're stuck with whatever ability level they currently have.

> This is exciting, because it means that to some extent, you can get out of this just by **deciding to have the other mindset**, in part by recognizing that all of the evidence you currently have is determined by the mindset you have and is thus untrustworthy as evidence of 'how things actually, fundamentally work'. That there's an explanation for the-experiences-that-come-with-fixed-mindset that makes sense in growth mindset too. So you can reinterpret everything and switch mindsets.

> *And*, it takes practice to actually *operate* from a growth mindset, rather than just conceptually understanding that it's a good idea to do so. In my experience, a lot of this practice can happen on the level of reframing verbal expression, where you can shift your language

from fixed to growth mindset. This in turn will shift your thoughts. That's what this post is about. The practice of thinking growthily.[2]

This, in turn, will change your thoughts. It's all about the practice of thinking growth. It's important always to think about growth, think positive and think forward. Fixed mindsets make it difficult to forge ahead. Growth mindsets profess anything is possible with positive thinking. Learning the difference between the two concepts will cause others to make calculated decisions about their lives.

Growth-minded leaders are the most progressive leaders to have. They speak of possibility and encourage others to think along the same vein. It's important to reach young people early with these concepts. Leaders know how to influence a growth mindset and teach forward-thinking ideas to help foster a positive environment. This doesn't mean everything will go right, but what it means is that those being influenced will practice upward and forward-thinking. Real leaders make positivity their first line of defense in all they do with those they've been assigned to lead.

It's also important to talk about the vehicle of leadership as a mobile effort. This is important since a vehicle represents mobility, and good leaders can move entrepreneurs and future leaders forward. Any leader who does not cause forward motion while keeping positive momentum helps to initiate stagnation. All leaders by right should be self-motivated to create future leaders to take over by positive influence and example.

As stated, leaders who do not solidify a united effort of teaching people to believe in themselves will not instill a sense of more profound pride. The growth mindset leader will trigger positive self-pride encouraging healthier mindsets and courageous actions. This type of leader not only creates the right kind of future leaders but deepens the motivation of the growth mindset follower. This brings positive outlooks, positive awareness and a thinking mindset to the follower. A sense of purpose and direction gives the growth mindset follower a future course to follow and directives to apply during the teaching and journey.

This kind of leadership ability is indeed sought after by business owners, corporations and even entrepreneurs. Leaders who create an environment for constant improvement and constant growth through positive life lessons and practical activities give the learning parties opportunities to show areas of growth and areas that may seem fixed. Once these areas are identified, it makes the leader's job more accessible because they now know where their followers are weak and where they are durable.

So, this brings us to understanding why individuals need to have leaders they trust and want to be trained and taught by. When the individuals involved trust the leader and how they are being led, this makes the leader's job more straightforward because there is a sense of confidence beyond the realm of dictatorship and authoritarianism — there is a mentor and mentee relationship.

There exists a tool that is very effective in influencing mindsets, and this takes us to the next concept.

For leaders, those chosen to lead and those who naturally lead in most situations that arise, it's vitally important to make sure the growth mindset is how such leaders want to influence those entrusted to their leadership abilities and skills. Making one's election and calling sure and trusting your position will bring about a healthy mindset and nurture those who will one day take a leadership position to lead others as they have been led. Leadership should never be taken lightly.

Choose to be the best leader possible. Take these steps and evaluate the leadership skills you possess. Leadership in today's world is sorely lacked amongst many. Some people are managers but not necessarily true leaders. It's essential to know the difference and be comfortable saying, 'I manage but need leadership training skills to lead those I've been entrusted to lead'. Take inventory of the skills you possess and see if while leading they foster positive influence amongst those you already may be leading.

NOTES

1. Maria Popova, 'Fixed vs. Growth: The Two Basic Mindsets That Shape Our Lives', Brain Pickings, https://www. brainpickings.org/2014/01/29/carol-dweck-mindset/, accessed 18 June 2020.

2. Malcolm Ocean, 'Two Ways to Make Your Language More Conducive to Growth Mindset', *Malcom* (blog), 24 July 2014, https://malcolmocean.com/2014/07/ growth-mindset-reframing/, accessed 18 June 2020.

Take Action

Ask yourself the following questions and then write your answers:

→ Am I leading with a growth mindset? Do I cause others to do the same? Where can I improve my leadership abilities, making them even more potent and valuable?

→ Who am I leading? Why am I leading them? How well am I leading? What exercises and training can I share to help those I lead to become stronger leaders of tomorrow?

→ What concepts can I incorporate in my leadership role that I have not already activated? What training may I need to add to my ability to lead in order to be even more effective going forward? Do I have a fixed mindset that may hinder my leadership abilities?

Chapter 2

LEADERSHIP REDEFINED

Let's go through this journey together.

First, let me try to describe leadership. I am not an expert; I have never claimed to be one. I am still learning. Some time ago I was in a classroom, and I was learning about change, leading change as an organisational renewal. There is where I heard my classmates calling me funny names like, 'the turnaround mae-stro'. It was then when I believed we had a conversation to hold. This is not about me – it's about us. I can suggest, but you can disagree, probably in between we would have a mid-course cry.

I will tell you a story: Some time ago I was in London with Linus Okorie. A great man came to speak, Chief Olusegun Obasanjo, and as he was at the podium, I was sitting next to him.

He was talking directly to me and I said to myself, 'Is it true that me, Ifie Sekibo, who was attending primary school when this man was the head of state of my nation, can be sitting here near him'? I was also to speak at the same podium; and when it was my turn I said,

> Since this great man has spoken, it will be difficult for small ones like us to say a thing. I need to remind him – and I want all of you who are slightly as old as I am to remember that Obasanjo put together what is called the 'leadership and citizenship instructions in schools'.

> In that former time, they sent soldiers to make sure we learnt. I thought when he later became president he would continue because those of us that had about two to three years of that programme were young. We were taught what a citizen of the country should do and shouldn't do, how we should behave, and more importantly, what our loyalty would mean for us as a country. Several years after this great man became head of state, they put together a constitution that made it difficult for those of us who were in that programme to be leaders of the country because we were too young to hold certain positions. This was done so that they could continue to lead us.

> Now, if we say tomorrow belongs to the youth but we put in our constitution age limits, that make it difficult for somebody who is less than forty to hold

certain positions – and essentially we are saying tomorrow belongs to the elders.

This is the first conversation I thought we should have about leadership. It goes back to the very essence of our country. Now, this may not sound very funny, though strange – I used to say that mine was the endangered generation. When I was younger I was too young to lead. Now I have grown to this level and I am too old to lead, because the world has moved. Meaning there is a generation of people who will never lead this country. All my life I have been in private enterprise and have been asked to share or lead a conversation that deals with vision and enterprise. We must encourage each generation at an early age to lead so they will have insight and enterprise to lead in business and other areas for the country's benefit.

VISION

Unfortunately, vision is nothing – attitude is everything. I have been in this visioning business for many years. I went to university for 4 years and had three solid years going back and forth to the campus of Harvard Business School. I studied theories that started hundreds of years ago that depend on vision. They taught us ordinary organisational things – vision, mission, core values. We wake up to write the vision, mission, and we forget the core values.

For there to be a vision, there has to be a human being willing to act on that vision. In the absence of an actively involved human being, vision is writing poetry. It starts with you, me, the person with the attitude to act. No matter how well educated you are, in the absence of you being present, there can be no vision. That presence transcends the sovereignty of a nation. That presence is in the human self.

What's the purpose of life? What's your goal? What do you seek to achieve as a person? It means you have to define yourself first. When you have identified yourself, then you can decide what to do. And if you relax knowing yourself, then you can sleep, and you can choose to dream; and if the dream is sweet, you can sleep again so that you can dream further. Unfortunately, like any other architect will do, he will paint a picture hoping humans will wake up and begin to put that picture together. So, vision is nothing; attitude is everything.

Indeed, anyone can follow instructions, anyone can create a vision, anybody can write about the image — but only one person can blaze the trail. That person is the leader. Leadership is an attitude subcell. *There are no known acts of leadership — there are attitudes to be developed.* If we can't improve the beliefs that have refrained some of us from being a mindset, if we don't define our mindset, we can kiss leadership goodbye, kiss visioning goodbye. We can't build. Give me the dullest team in this world, and with the right attitude, we can do great things if every one of them chooses to change their mindset.

When I talk with my colleagues at Heritage Bank, I tell jokes, but leadership is no joke. Those of us who read the Bible know God was worried only one time, and that's when every mind was bent on building a structure to see Him upstairs, in heaven (Genesis 11:1-9). God essentially said, 'If I leave them with this one mind of theirs, they will achieve what they set out to do. The best way to stop them is to let them be divided in their thinking, in their language'. God understands that people with one vision can be unstoppable. That is the power of the brain and its capability.

ATTITUDE

Our attitude determines our approach to life; our attitude determines our relationship with people; our position is also the difference between our success and failures. Our philosophy is a function of how we start a task and how we conclude that task. Indeed, our attitude can turn a problem to a blessing. Leaders have a tenacious attitude. Where does the word 'persistence' come from? It comes from the definition of an entrepreneur. Most people define an entrepreneur as a risk taker but that is not correct — it is actually the person who relentlessly pursues opportunities without regard to current resources, which means partnership.

Leadership involves

- building partnerships,

- building teams,

- building like minds,

- building people around you, giving them the confidence they need and

- helping people redefine themselves, letting them see that they are better than you are only if they dare to stand and face the question as you are viewing it.

Leadership is the ability to get people to believe in themselves, not you. They have the power to be able to do it if they know they can do it. Then, they can join with you to do it. A team will do it. No one person can build an organisation. No matter how wealthy, how educated and how influential you are – you need a team.

Forward-thinking organisations believe small and medium scale enterprises hold the future of Nigeria, but then we must be able to let them discover themselves. We built the Small and Medium Enterprises (SME) Clinic at the inception of Heritage Bank. The reason for the SME Clinic is simple – to get people to agree that they are the solutions to their situations. One person can never build an organisation, you need people to cooperate to build an organisation. That cooperation is not a vision, that cooperation is a mindset; it's an attitude issue. In my estimation, we have succeeded in a few, but we need a critical mass to make a difference.

THE DOWNSIDES OF COOPERATION

Competition, not necessarily cooperation, is what drives us to excel. For example, why did Usain Bolt want to break the 100-metre record of 9.9 seconds? It is because of competition. If there weren't people who could do 9.9 seconds, you wouldn't go for 9.58 seconds, which he did. Because he knew someone ran 100 metres in 9.9 seconds, he did his best to run faster and break that record. When we talk about healthy competition, we talk about having respect for the person who set the record – which motivates us to want to set a better record ourselves.

Cooperation, on the other hand, sometimes leads to docility, leads to apathy, leads to a laissez-faire attitude and makes people comfortable with just getting by. It supports the 'It doesn't matter whether I do the work or not, I'll still pass' attitude among students.

In every sphere of business and every industry, you must cooperate in setting the rules of the game – the boundaries within which we need to compete. The absence of cooperation for a level playing field, if there can be such, is like a football match. If you go outside the boundaries, competition becomes unhealthy. An unhealthy competition gives rise to the downward trends of the gains you would have made if you competed in a healthy environment.

The reason why you see people push governments to put structures and institutions that will encourage healthy competition is that favouritism can happen under the guise of cooperation. You need a high level of cooperation to set the boundaries within which competition should take place. That is the nexus between competition and cooperation. In the absence of cooperation, what you find is chaos; and in the presence of unhealthy competition, what you find is regression, not progression.

This important balance is even evident in the animal kingdom. I was opportune to watch a group of meerkats cooperating. Whenever an eagle is coming, one meerkat will give the alarm, and all the other meerkats will take cover. Still, conflicts between meerkat 'clans' are common — they sometimes fight for food and other resources. At the point of the food, there is competition, at the point of collective threat from external aggression, there is cooperation. The boundaries are essential to prevent cheating.

PARTNERSHIPS

I ask people when I make presentations, how is it that there has never been, for over one hundred years of Nigeria or more, an organisation that has transitioned from one generation to the next? It's because we believe that one man is the owner. He wants to be the alpha, the secretary, treasurer and everything. But if he goes away, the second generation kills it because they were not part of the mindset. They had no vested interest in the business or organisation.

For us to see a future of enterprises being built that will give rise to a greater tomorrow, leaders must step forth now and seek partnerships and cooperation from others to build a future. This was the SME Clinic's primary goal.

Today's leaders must begin to change the 'one man' mindset to a together mindset. People always focus on wanting to get rich. First, that's the wrong concept; instead, they should seek to get wealth. Wealth is everywhere in this country. If only our leaders knew this. Look for somewhere to release the asset, find people who can lend the asset to you, so you don't waste your money. In that collaboration, you own your bit, and we all play our part. We can transmit to the next group of people. It doesn't have to be my child, but the future human beings who will have the same mindset. As we grow, we are teaching those younger than us the same method of building. When we ease out of the me-only mindset, the next generations will continue the process. And the nation will begin to have generational organisations.

I dared all who were present for my talk to point out to me any organisation in Nigeria, owned by Nigerians, that has continued beyond one generation. I know of one founded in Dublin that may come to mind – the brewery company, Guinness. Actually, the Guinness family now owns only about 2 or 3 percent of that organisation, yet it is preserved for future generations. We work for today, we create riches for today – they create wealth for tomorrow. Until we change our 'today' visioning mindset and begin to develop enterprises for 'tomorrow', there is no future to be given to the youth.

The leadership journey and discussion have to start with the fundamentals of training young people. Leaders should be prepared to ask and answer questions such as, 'What do you need from me? An autograph or money?' Since money might overwhelm children, maybe a unique signature would make them better people tomorrow. Perhaps that's why I am trying to postulate that people begin to create a name for themselves and an 'autograph' at the end. I prefer the term 'autograph' rather than 'legacy' as it implies a person's unique signature – a specific identity associated with an individual.

I was in the USA, leaving the airport in Philadelphia, Pennsylvania, going to the University of Pennsylvania, and I saw a massive billboard. Do you know what was written on it? Nothing. Its red background hosted a white outline of Nelson Mandela's face. He was a South African – not an American. So, why the large signage? It sends the message that he didn't fight for himself. He fought for a generation who never knew him or met him, but he left his autograph for them.

So, what is your concept of legacy, your autograph? I think that legacy is the one thing that everyone should strive towards – to make your special mark on the world, starting with your home, then business, etc. No matter your concept of leadership, there lies your legacy, your autograph. You can write a book just because you saw Nelson Mandela. You can discuss compromise, freedom, revolution, politics, philanthropy and you can discuss anything. An autograph is a collection of the entity of human engagement. When people look at me and say an organisation is a legacy, I say, 'No, the legacy is the human endeavour, the person'.

The human being is the most substantial economic force in the world. Whatever you build is driven by humans; and if they do not have the right mindset, real progress will continue to be a mirage. Organisations do not become the best by themselves, but can become the best if the individuals driving them have the necessary mindset to make it so. This is why I say vision is nothing without the right attitude or mindset to push it to fulfillment.

You can't change a mindset without demanding it to define the problem; so, the easiest way to see someone's mindset is to have them identify the problem. As they do, they see their limitations and you can begin to influence them positively. It is essential in our efforts to change the outlook of our youth, to get them out of the mindset that they have to be the best or have all the resources to be good enough.

Many are stuck in this rut and won't overcome until they are mentored out of it. We must get them to transcend their current circumstances and keep their eyes on the goals they want to achieve. We must train them to think optimally, which is when the human mind looks beyond itself to succeed. The culture or mindset of self that is prevalent in the youth of today must be changed to a mentality of us and we. We must deliberately begin to eliminate the 'I' and replace it with 'we' if we are to see the economic, political and social transformation we so desire.

SHARING THE OPPORTUNITIES

In addition to teamwork, mindset, vision and attitude, another critical factor in the leadership success equation is to develop the skill of sharing opportunities, giving the work to others to accomplish. Good leaders have a habit of generating the idea and then giving it to others to execute while watching from a distance and pulling the right strings. By doing so, you provide opportunities for others to experience leadership and to refine their attitudes until they become the type of persons they can be.

I believe that there is a misunderstanding responsible for delaying Africa's global recognition. A lot of Africans miss the mark by defining themselves in a context of others and not themselves. Africans must begin to *replace the concept of globalisation with glocalisation,* which is merely being local with a global perception. In my opinion, glocalisation is the art of influencing, empowering and developing our local systems to worldwide recognition.

We must first succeed in attracting attention in our personal, our local, social space before reaching out globally. Only when people see our local success will they invite us to share our success and see how they can apply it to their situation. Only then will our success become global. Africans must localise their success first before seeking global attention. Charity, they say, begins at home. We must define ourselves in the context of our Africanness before we can attract global recognition.

I believe that the individual is central to any vision or nation building. We must refine the minds of the younger generation to draw out the good in each special young person. We do this by mentoring and teaching them how to think optimally. When they are challenged to think perpetually, they can build generational organisations that provide not only lasting wealth and assure sustainable development to and for future generations, but also offer global recognition.

A CHALLENGE TO YOUNG GENERATIONS

In this modern high-tech era, many young people say they want to be global leaders. They say distance is dead and globalisation is the way to success. For the young people who say they want to be global leaders, the following advice will help them achieve their aspirations.

First, you can't give what you don't have. It's not an impossible task to achieve, but what are you bringing to the table? Are you just bringing the hope of, 'I'm a leader', to the table? Or, are you bringing 'idea generation' and a set of paradigms that can shine like beacons, like a lighthouse, to the table? If you're not bringing anything of substance to the table and you only have a copycat vision, you will not become a leader. After all, anybody can call themselves a leader. It takes much more to actually become a person who leads.

Global leadership is nothing but one set of people imposing their rules of engagement on others; based on ideas, based on superiority in terms of wealth creation, and all the likes. But I push all those back in my submission and would rather you say, 'I don't want to be a *global* leader, I want to be a *glocal* leader'. Let your *local* leadership transmit and catapult you into *global* relevance. Say rather, 'I don't want to leave Nigeria and go to the UN and become a senator because I am educated – I want my community and larger communities to recognise my touch of compassion for human life and my desire to help them improve their sustenance and essence; to give them a better life in every aspect. Let that be a projection on which the global stage touches me'.

For example, a young Bangladeshi economist became a global leader by founding a grassroots bank that addressed the poverty and housing problems of his country and became a microfinancing pioneer focused on helping women and young people. He was a *glocal* leader first. He said, 'Young people … should learn that there are two kinds of businesses in the world. One is a business which makes money, and the other solves the problems of the world. It's an academic exercise and what they do with that in real life will depend on them, what kind of life they would like to choose'.[1]

Glocalisation, rather than globalisation, is your ability to influence your local community for the greater good, to impact your ideas and your way of doing things to the larger society and the larger world makes you a leader on the global stage. That is the essence of true leadership; that you impact your local community for a wider benefit. People will acknowledge your local community success, seeing all the idiosyncrasies and factors that you managed and then adapt their circumstances or situations in their communities. You will be called to have a conversation with them and you will have references in your local area that will attest to your successful endeavours.

I share the example of Jack Ma, the cofounder of Alibaba, telling his story. He says by the time Alibaba was emerging, there were big organisations like Apple and Google already on the scene. So all the 'best brains' were taken and he was left with people who weren't hired by Google and Apple. But he grew his e-commerce business into one of the largest organisations in the world because he influenced and stayed true to the local community and allowed the local community to see him as part of them. He grew with them, saw that their fate was tied to his fate and they believed in him as a leader. They stayed with him as he built the business from the ground up. Today, 20 years later, he could buy 5 Googles, 3 Facebooks, Amazon or whatever. His net worth is more than $40 billion, and he retired in 2019 when he was 55 years old. He did not set out to be a global leader, he set out to be a local leader. It is local leadership that gives a person global attention.

NOTE

1. Miriam Cosic, '"We Are All Entrepreneurs": Muhammad Yunus on changing the world, one microloan at a time', *The Guardian*, 29 March 2017, https://www.theguardian.com/sustainable-business/2017/mar/29/we-are-all-entrepreneurs-muhammad-yunus-on-changing-the-world-one-microloan-at-a-time; accessed 24 June 2020.

Take Action

Ask yourself the following questions and then write your answers:

➡ Am I leading with a growth mindset or a fixed mindset? Which is best to accomplish the goal?

➡ Do I cause others to think with a growth mindset? If not, what steps can I take to promote that mindset in others?

➡ How can I improve my leadership abilities, making them even more potent and valuable?

➡ Are my contributions relevant to my local community?

Chapter 3

The Fifth Sense – Emotional Intelligence

In Nigeria, Africa, and some parts of Europe and the USA, we seem to have a very wrong connotation about someone visiting a psychologist regarding the condition of their mental health. In Nigeria, if you are under deep contemplation and you seek advice to have that conversation with a psychologist or psychiatrist, some people think you are not 'normal'. In an advanced world with pressures, emotions are assaulted at work and private life, and they all dovetail into how much you apply yourself to dealing with others.

I wrote a poem that I gave to my staff that discusses the important things we needed to say to each other, such as, 'I love you'.

Some wondered why I had to write it for my organisation. I was trying to tell a story, and my account was simple: we wake up in the morning, we say goodbye to our families, we go to the office where we spend 8-12 hours and we return to our homes. If we don't understand the pressure we take from the workplace to the house and vice versa, we find ourselves out of balance, we become irritable, unteachable, irrational and a lot of negativity starts to come into play.

Now if you don't understand that there is continual bouncing between those who we are at home and the workplace, you are unable to articulate whether you have a sound mind. So in terms of trying to have that balance — that 'oh, I need to do my work in a particular way because my emotions are relating proportionally to the pressure I get from work' — such understanding is critical to how you succeed or do not succeed, because it is an organisational behaviour issue.

Organisational behaviour, which has become a serious area of study, is rooted in emotional intelligence that includes knowing the

- personality traits of each individual at work,
- team dynamics you form and
- personality traits of members functioning as a group.

Organisation behaviour also includes understanding the strongest as well as the weakest persons within your organisation, and how you treat the weakest person on the team is important. How do you support and motivate that person to appreciate his strengths even when he seems to be weak? As the strongest on the team, how do you relate to the less secure people within the organisation? All these daily interactions count when leading a productive and cohesive team.

These are conflict issues we need to know how to manage; and if you do not have empathy or sympathy in the creation of a team, then there will always be a disconnect. If you read leadership books on teaming, you will see that there are two stages: the formation stage and the storming stage. The storming stage is the most critical stage, where first you form the team believing they will work together – then the storming comes when personalities clash.

Those with good emotional intelligence adjust and survive, while those who don't could allow issues to fester to the point where the idea is destroyed. Of course, there is the issue of leadership within the team. The initial person appointed to be the leader of the group may not necessarily have wanted that position, but was legislated into it. If that leader doesn't appreciate the stress of the others in the team or the organisation, he may not have balance in his emotional arrangement.

There are lots of things that happen in leadership that start from an individual's personality, to the personality of the team, to the character of the organisation, to the nature of the outside world – and if you can't balance competing needs, you have chaos, and many have ended up with serious mental health problems.

The concept of leaving traceable impact as a result of the positive feelings you deposit in the lives of those who cross your path is what inspires them to seek to be more. A former President of the USA, John Quincy Adams, said, 'If your actions inspire others to dream more, learn more, do more and become more, you are a leader'. This is so true. Experts are beginning to conclude that the more likable a leader is, the more influence the leader will possess. Organisations that have a culture of love, a culture of looking after one another, organisations that are committed to personal effectiveness and wellness and welfare of staff, usually make more progress than those who do not have that positive work environment. That is why Martin Luther King Jr. said, 'Everybody can be great, because anybody can serve….You don't have to know the second theory of thermodynamics in physics to serve. You only need a heart full of grace, a soul generated by love'.

When leaders promote love within their institutions, within their families, within their organisations, what happens usually is that they get the deposits of the love back as well. For any leader to make tremendous and significant progress, the leader must be a lover of people, the leader must be someone who gives love, gives hope, inspires and adds value to other people. These are deposits that can be cashed in at any point in time. The more you give of every concept of love, the more you will understand how to deal with human beings.

Every human has a temperament. Every human has strengths and weaknesses. Every human has a personal background.

Every human is a unique individual. What I'm talking about here is the ability of the leader to be sensitive enough to 1) understand the individuality of humanity as a whole; 2) understand what makes each member of the team special; 3) understand the values they all share; and 4) reprogram or adjust plans and procedures to deal with these human beings in a way that leaves a printable autograph in their hearts.

The lack of emotional intelligence within institutions and in a lot of families has caused so much distraction that we must now take the reality of emotional intelligence very seriously. There are components of emotional intelligence that have to do with how human beings connect with each other through heartfelt love. Simon Sinek wrote a book, *Leaders Eat Last;* and in that book, one of the major themes is how leaders, through the effective understanding of emotional intelligence, can decide to think less of themselves and put their followers ahead of them when benefits accrue for all involved.

Leaders who leave lasting legacies first think of their followers – how they can solve real problems for them. When followers see this attribute consistently over time, they begin to endear leaders who love, care, show attention and respect the feelings of others. Leaders who deposit positive things in the lives of those who work for them and with them will reap the rewards of loyalty and productivity.

Emotional intelligence also includes the way we communicate with the people we work with. If we are known to shout at people – at work or at home – they will presume we do not really care about their feelings. Rather than being aggressive, we can talk to them in an assertive way and present our thoughts kindly, not harshly. At the end of the day, what we are simply practicing is emotional intelligence – handling our emotions intelligently for the good of others and ourselves.

For instance, a staff member or a team that has been consistently committed over an extended period of time suddenly develops an attitude that is totally different from what the staff has been known for. They may be quiet or even look depressed. A leader with emotional intelligence has the ability to figure out why the staff is behaving differently and will address the issue and get the staff back on track. Most changes in behaviour are because the general feeling within organisations is that leaders don't care. That feeling is so strong that it impacts the staff's ability to produce and be productive all the time. So, the principle of emotional intelligence becomes a priority in terms of ranking on the list of skills leaders must have.

MODELS OF LEADERSHIP

To become a leader who will be remembered, loved and celebrated, is to follow the path of developing emotional intelligence so that your influence can outlive you as an individual. Therefore, I suggest we begin to evaluate the models of leadership that we are pursuing. Are we promoting fear within the organisation so people will be scared of us? Or, are we intimidating the staff or manipulating the staff? Fear, intimidation and manipulation will not generate the response you desire — you will not generate influence.

Take for instance the story about a woman who was interviewed many years ago about her experience one evening with two former Prime Ministers of England — Benjamin Disraeli and William Gladstone. She was asked about her impression of these two great men and the woman said, 'When I left the dining room after sitting next to Mr Gladstone, I thought he was the cleverest man in England. But after sitting next to Mr Disraeli, I thought I was the cleverest woman in England'.

This means that people will never forget how you make them feel or how you actually impacted them. When you are actually interested in other people, they will remember you long after the time spent with them.

ARE LEADERS HOPE DEALERS?

I like Mariah Carey's song in which she sings, 'If there's one spark of hope left in my grasp I'll hold it with both hands'. There is power in hope. There is enormous spiritual, physical, psychological power in hope. A strand of hope is better than anything else when we face a point of crisis.

There are many cases worldwide where the only reason people survived, the only reason the organisation didn't fail, was because there was hope. Hope that a shut door might just be kicked open, a wind might just blow to make the only fruit on a tree fall for us to grab it. It's so important that you keep hope alive. It may sound like a cliché, but underneath the cliché is the gospel truth that every human endeavour was once a hope to be achieved and obtained.

Where there is no hope, the human spirit dies. The only reason why we go back to vote in another election, or we believe society will change, is because we have one strand of hope. Just one more try and we can make it better.

Your life can be better with just one more try. Relentlessly pursue an opportunity, and you will generate the hope that you will make it. You go to school, there is a hope you will make it. You jump into a river, there is a hope you will swim across, especially in shark-infested waters. So, hope is a potent and powerful ingredient of success when you hit a crisis block.

In the African wild — as in human life — the path to where antelopes, bulls, cows and sheep could all drink during a dry season is fret with crocodiles, lions, alligators and all kinds of dangerous animals. Yet they all instinctively travel that long journey to a greater haven because they have hope. They know some of them will be eaten by predators. When they wake up in the morning, the lions will run to find food else they will die hungry. And all the small animals will run else they become food for the lions. So there is daily running, every animal and everybody must run — and the end of the race is uncertain. Every race is an uncertain race, to the point where even a lion in the race to catch a buffalo may be killed. Even the king of the forest, who thinks he's the strongest, sometimes gets maimed and killed in the process of the migration. You could have thought it certain that a lion would always capture a buffalo or an antelope to eat, but all it takes is for the buffalo or antelope to put its horn through the lion's jaw and the lion is dead; the lion becomes meat for other animals to eat. So we cannot say there is a recipe for uncertainty.

Knowing that, I judge some situations as being favourable opportunites and others unfavourable. Favourable to the extent that you know what you want and you go for it. You calculate your risks for what it's worth and believe it's what you want. You must put your best foot forward approaching that opportunity, in fact every opportunity you consider favourable. It doesn't matter whether it's in your own local community, or Africa, Asia or Europe, for each and every interaction you choose to make, determine to present yourself as the best option among the others vying for the opportunity.

If it's a negotiation that is worth everybody's while, hope that everyone involved will reach an agreement where all are happy. But realise that 90 percent of the time, not all are happy. Knowing with certainty that you'll be happy at the end of a deal is not guaranteed. Would you rather have a deal or no deal? From my years of experience, sometimes no deal is a good deal. Is it certain that you will have a no deal? No. Sometimes, even when you don't want a deal, a deal will be forced on you and it might turn out to be a good deal. So the bottom line is, as uncertain as opportunities are, it's also the joy of life. I call uncertainty the spice that makes life worth the living!

Therein lies your ability to display character, courage, humanity, fairness, openness, and to make others realise that the colour of your skin has no place in you being you; you can be you wherever you go, because it's in the content of your character and not in the colour of your skin or eyes, which Martin Luther King Jr. stated so elequotently.

Humanity is essentially the same; we all face challenges, we all face uncertainties and we all face issues to deal with. How we face our daily life ends up exposing our sense of character, our ability to understand the issues on the table and our ability to appreciate the humanness of the person across the table. Sometimes the humanness seems nonexistent, yet you need to display your humanity, your integrity in every instance as a leader.

Take Action

Ask yourself the following questions and then write your answers:

- Am I an emotionally intelligent person? If yes, explain. If no, why not? How can you increase your emotional intelligence?

- Do I cause others to become emotionally intelligent? If not, what steps can I take to promote that mindset in them?

- What impressions do people have of me? What impressions would I like people to have of me?

- Do I engender 'hope' in the uncertainty surrounding circumstances I face with my team? If yes, how? If not, what steps can I take to sell hope?

Chapter 4

FAITH – THE SUCCESS TRIGGER

I firmly believe that faith enables your business to be successful, and faith in God gives meaning and purpose to human life.

Faith in God is the basis for every other add-on – it gives value to human life. Faith in a supreme being is setting the boundary to your life's existence so you can approach your fellow man with human understanding and build the interactions needed to make a business succeed. Faith is the only thing you can't live without; everything else is an addition.

I want to emphasise that your faith is what you base your life on – it's the foundation on which you stand. For instance, if I want to go to hell, all my activities are driven towards that end. To a large extent, people of faith are influenced by their faith in everything they do. If, for example, I have a genre of faith in Mohammed, I would observe and believe what he did right, and this belief would become important in the way I do business. If I am a Christian, certain ethical values become critical to my success as a person, and my human engagement would be driven by that.

So, faith drives our human engagement. I believe and hope you will too, that 90 percent of leadership is done in faith. If you have no values, you can't be a leader. Bad is the absence of good; you can't define bad where there is no good — so if your faith has helped you to desire good, you can almost always distinguish bad.

FAITH AND FEAR

We can learn a lesson from Julius Caesar. No Roman general was allowed to cross the Rubicon, a river separating the province of Gaul from Rome. By the rules of engagement he could not cross, because this would have meant treason and/or a declaration of war against the state. I have read over and over all the analysis, stories and the conjectures of why Caesar broke the rule. He didn't break the rule because he wanted to — his life and the lives of his army were at stake. To me, it's daring and beating the odds. Likewise, when the life of an organisation is at stake, the leader needs to take actions that will safeguard its resources. Survival was part of Caesar's principles.

His thought was that he himself and fear were two lions jostling for glory, and eventually only the fiercest of the two would survive. By crossing the Rubicon, he showed that he was fiercer than fear. So, what that tells me is that courage is not the absence of fear, but taking action despite fear.

Again, Julius Caesar confronted similar impossible circumstances and dared them. A case in point is his movement from Rome to what is Spain today. The two locations were separated by the Alps, the most rugged mountain range in the middle of Europe. Against all odds, he managed to march a troop of nearly a million men through the Alps to the doorstep of his enemy when they least expected him.

I can only imagine the pain, the courage and perhaps the ingenuity it took at a time when there were no bulldozers or tractors to break through the Alps and get to the other side.

Today, there is the Mont Blanc Tunnel that links France and Italy and there are roads, but back in 50 BCE one man, Julius Caesar, thought it was possible to break through the mountain, arrive at his enemy's gate and conquer the region.

Therein lies the essence of leadership – not physical attributes, but internal qualities a leader must possess, including faith in yourself and courage. Courage is one of those internal qualities and also a scarce commodity: 'Courage is not the absence of fear but despite fear, stepping forward'.

Courage is not foolishness, such as if somebody is pointing a gun at your head and you say go ahead and shoot. You are not courageous, you are foolish, because you must stay alive. My friends normally say in times of war, 'Stay alive. You can be injured, but stay alive. The injured can be treated, the dead will be buried'. So, courage is when facing challenges, you dare them, but with enough skill to still keep yourself alive.

Julius Caesar portrayed all of the qualities of leadership — yes, even in his state of greatness, he admitted his failing and inadequateness. When Caesar was in his early 30s, he saw the statue of Alexander the Great in Egypt and wept; at his age, the Macedonian king had already conquered the known world, while Caesar still struggled to conquer Europe. Indeed, somebody is looking at you, is he somebody greater than you?

It doesn't matter how old you are, you still have something to learn and there is something greater than you that you cannot easily ignore. So, I always distinguish the entrepreneur as the leader, but there are always leaders within leadership. I also look up to others as my leaders, such as the chairman of my board is my leader.

OWN THE OPPORTUNITY

Entrepreneurship or leadership can be interchanged in any form and shape. I believe entrepreneurship exposes leaders, not a leader. Entrepreneurship exposes leaders in various areas of endeavour — in micro and macro groups — that create and expose other leaders who will go into different spheres of life, taking from what they have done. A simple example is the evolution of 'fintech' – financial technology. Fintech happened when people, including Bill Gates who had faith in his idea, were trying to create organisations as entrepreneurs. Fintech lashed onto the World Wide Web (WWW), that morphed into thousands of startup companies aimed at using computers and smartphones for banking and financial services. From there, tech companies including Yahoo, Facebook, Twitter, Twitter, Instagram, WhatsApp and millions more, were born And each of these businesses are led by entrepreneurs who have grabbed hold of another person's innovation and came up as leaders. Today, Jack Ma, cofounder of Alibaba, is worth more than $40 billion. There was nothing original about his financial e-business, but he became a very strong leader in the fintech world.

So, who is an entrepreneur and who is the real leader? I call leadership and entrepreneurship interchangeable words that people use without much thought, almost like a whirlpool where the same water can go in and be thrown out. Meaning, that at different times and in different circumstances, various leaders emerge. And as they emerge, they will cause disruption, which can cause innovation. And one innovation will cause another innovation to happen, one disruption will cause another disruption to happen, and so leaders will continue to emerge here and there. When they surface, the factors of leadership do not change.

You label someone an entrepreneur, a business person, a risk taker, whatever it is, and they all pursue opportunities.

But some do not pursue opportunity and own it. Those who own the opportunities can seriously be called leaders. Leaders own each opportunity, grab the vision, have faith in the vision and run with it.

One time when I was speaking in a business forum in a church I said, 'I can't understand how a pastor can preach prosperity and he's not prospering himself, or can teach leadership and cannot lead himself'. The reason is simple. People can read it and know it, but they don't have what it takes to grab it and internalise it — make it their own by faith. You have to internalise the vision, have faith in it. The entrepreneur who does not internalise his or her own vision and sees it as just a money-making venture will never be a leader.

You have to internalise the vision and recognise all the various aspects of leadership in life. Leadership becomes part of everyday life for a leader. If you don't accept leadership responsibilities and its inherent ramifications, chances are you will end up being a visionary or a dreamer — not an entrepreneur or a leader.

Take Action

Ask yourself the following questions and then write your answers:

➡ How much faith do I have in my vision? Does my faith stand strong amid disruptions?

➡ Do I stir faith in others to see my vision? What steps can I take to stir up their faith?

➡ How can I make my faith stronger?

Chapter 5

OPTIMAL THINKING

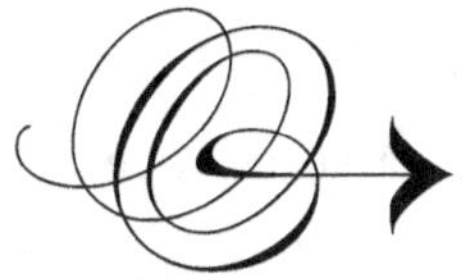

For the past thirty years or more, people have ridden on the back of 'positive thinking', believing if they think positively, they will achieve. It's become a kind of refrain or mantra that people use to psych themselves into action. This mindset has its root in the Bible, anything you set your mind to do you will do.

What happens in thinking positively is that you push forward even in the face of challenges and issues by reminding yourself that some of your achievements of today were challenges yesterday. So, what we thought we would not be able to do or achieve has already been done and produced by us. Every issue that was very important and strategically key, we took time to address to the logical conclusion.

In our efforts to revive SGBN, it will shock you to know that in just one day, over two hundred court cases by customers on the bank were withdrawn entirely from the court and settled. It was unbelievable – and a huge stride in the right direction due to optimal thinking.

The total value of those cases was pegged at over thirty billion (30,000,000,000) naira, and were settled in just one day by my team. All thanks to optimal thinking. Optimal thinking is about being your best and doing your best to achieve a set goal or objective. Its value can't be overly quantified for any right-thinking organisation or individual to attain its objectives and achieve its vision, mission and maximise profit.

Optimal thinking is not just about positive thinking – it goes beyond that. It is vital to have a positive outlook, but positive thinking alone is not sufficient to guarantee success. You discover that most positive thinkers, when confronted with challenges and obstacles, usually have no tenacity to continue being positive. Giving up and becoming negative is opposed to optimal thinking, which is defying the odds to achieve success.

Optimal thinking is about being the best of yourself and coming up with the best solutions. Regardless of what kind of trials and problems you must tackle in the business day, irrespective of how challenging you find the situation and even if those circumstances become tougher, there is always a step you can take in the right, positive direction.

There is also the ideal decision available to you, which we can call an optimal choice. When using your brain's thought process, there are some very fundamental levels of mentality you work with: negative and suboptimal thinking as well as positive thinking.

NEGATIVE AND SUBOPTIMAL THINKING

The victim mindset and negative thinking are suboptimal ways of viewing daily challenges and are often based on giving your power away, wholly. This type of thinking brings with it low self-esteem, no confidence, bleakness and feelings of vulnerability.

A suboptimal belief system means your way of thinking is mediocre, average and only sometimes positive. So when a very challenging job requires your best decision-making thinking, the best you will do is average.

Optimal views and thinking are the opposite of a victim mindset and a negative method of thinking. Learning to adapt to thinking more optimally will lead to more optimal choices you will make, which leads you to the most exceptional outcomes possible! You will attain your goals with more efficiency, giving you a feeling of satisfaction and positive attitude.

Optimal thinking teaches how to heal from a victim mindset that keeps people from succeeding. Thinking like a victim — life isn't fair, you've been taken advantage of, feeling sorry for yourself, thinking you missed the boat and there is no hope — will take you down and keep you there for life. A negative thought process includes a thick chain around your neck. But as you become more acquainted with thinking optimally, you will take more ideal actions more consistently, giving you a better quality of life. No more feeling inadequate about your abilities. You will become super productive as you learn to depend on your best self.

There is another way of thinking – suboptimal thinking. Though it doesn't debilitate you, it does make you feel okay in your comfort zone. There is where you never have to stretch yourself in any way to do more or be more than you know deep down that you could be. It leads to feeling okay with living an average life. Suboptimal thinking stagnates people: sitting on the sofa, letting life go by, living in a rut. This is where most people fail. There is a beautiful little proverb that is so true: 'As a man thinks, so is he'. In other words, you are what you think.

Napoleon Hill said, 'Whatever the mind of man can conceive and believe, it can achieve'. Write that down on an index card and tape it where you will see it day in and day out. There is no better reminder of how capable and reliable you are.

But if a mediocre life isn't good enough for the kind of lifestyle you envision in your dreams, then you must learn to think differently. If you want to attain your crowning potential, you merely have to elevate your thinking from 'typical' to becoming the 'best' version of yourself.

Here's what to do: You must start by asking yourself the correct questions. That's the only way to train your mind to look for the very best result all the time, every time. 'Only the best' is the top solution and method to incorporate optimal thinking in your life.

At first, altering your 'normal' thinking is challenging to do. You are telling your mind it has to learn something different from what it was used to for so long. It's human nature to fight change in many areas of life. It's just not a good feeling to suddenly force change on your mind and body. It revolts for a while until your psyche is convinced you are serious.

Scientists have proven that our brains have a plasticity that enables us to reroute old, hurtful thinking patterns from harmful situations we have experienced. When old thoughts about circumstances that caused a victim way of thinking arise, we replace those negative, destructive memories with thoughts of joyous experiences. When we keep doing that for an extended length of time, soon those hurtful memories will take a far back seat. Once we thought we were stuck with our thoughts; we now know that is not the truth — what a fantastic reality!

AIM FOR BEST

Every decision, every plan you are asked to implement, everything you want to create or fix or make better, you must ask yourself, 'What is the best way to…?' in order to do or get done whatever the challenge or job is before you. By asking yourself, 'What is best…?' you are raising your standards psychologically and emotionally. You will also start searching for totally new solutions you never thought about before. You will actually feel yourself expanding new ideas, accomplishing more than ever.

Implementing the optimal manner of thinking and decision making will bless your life with increased self-confidence, a greater sense of self-esteem and self-respect. You will begin to believe in yourself; believing that nothing is impossible if you want it badly enough.

This is the time to be determined that you can have more out of life because you deserve it. Know that. Believe it. Remind yourself constantly.

Take Action

This is where the rubber meets the road as the saying goes. Ideas without action are like making a meal and throwing it in the garbage; it does you no good at all. You're still hungry. So, pull up your boots and get to work. The final results will be amazing. And this new way of decision making will soon become second nature to the point that it will seem like you never lived any other way.

➡ What is the main reason why thinking optimally is not second nature to us? You must be able to manage your emotions. Learning to live a more satisfying life with optimal decision making means your reasoning powers cannot be obscured with overpowering thoughts of negativity. Being in tune with your emotions is like a compass guiding you which way to go. You are in charge.

➡ Ignoring your feelings is the number one reason why people never achieve optimal thinking to make the best decisions for success. Get to know that inner voice — it's not always on your side. We must become the master of our mind and body. Nothing changes without a lot of hard work and determination. And nothing is so satisfying as reaching goals.

➡ Precept upon precept, line upon line, slowly is the best way to learn hard things. Practice makes perfect isn't some silly maxim, but a truth. Learn one right action like being in control of your thinking or asking how you can best learn to use optimal thinking — and repeat that tenet until it's a solid habit. Then, go on to the next and then into the future until you reach success! For exceptional outcomes, you need to take extraordinary measures. To take outstanding actions, you have to learn to think in unconventional ways.

Chapter 6

THE REFINERY

The most powerful economic force is the human being, or the economics of the human being. The primary resource of every business, organisation or country – profit-making or not – is the human being. Each human by default is wired with the innate ability to do good and to be good. However, externalities – situational things – could influence them towards the wrong direction. These externalities serve as roadblocks and often prohibit us from bringing out the good that is within us.

OIL AND HUMANS

A perfect illustration is in the drilling of crude oil, which takes a lot of effort. The process involves drilling deep down and bringing up the black gold. After that, this black gold needs to be refined to become useful. In refining the crude oil, it takes on forms that are distinctly different from its raw state.

Likewise, at the point when students finish their university education, they believe they have some understanding they didn't have before. They graduate with a Bachelor's degree in Economics or Accounting or any other field of study, but they still may be unaware of all the potential still remaining inside. This fact ignited a thought in me to build a refinery and pass these people through it and expose them to greater opportunities to blossom; this would assist them to understand who they actually are. So I built a refining, or training, school. Upon entering, I warn them that what they learn will affect every one of their relationships — because they will exit as entirely different people. They spend a total of six months learning the best ways to think, behave and perceive the world around them and beyond.

My concept of refinery is exposing the human mind to a myriad of possibilities. Young people attending the refinery are trained to accept the possibilities that life can present. In between, we teach them some elements of banking; but most importantly, we teach them poise, dating, social interactions, law, leadership and all kinds of subjects that are not part of traditional bank training.

I encourage the students to take a photograph of themselves the first day and take another on graduation day to see the difference between the two. Every year, they observe that not one person has looked the same. I do this for them to appreciate the interdependence between themselves and their colleagues. It is exciting to see how the human mind can be moulded and influenced to do things that it thought impossible. Most of the people who pass through the refinery, graduate with stories of how they couldn't do certain things before, but can after the training and this gives me joy.

I tell them that they have the potential to someday be a managing director of a bank and then teach them the qualities needed to become a managing director. I instruct them about thinking optimally, having an attitude of leadership, respecting followership, adding value, implementing a best-life view and most of all to be willing to take responsibility for wrong steps, if they want to be leaders. So, for example, a refined person to me is someone that having studied law asks to be posted to a department other than the legal department as a result of the different interests developed while in the training school.

REFINEMENT IS A FULL-TIME JOB

We must continuously refine the minds of the youth to harness the beautiful treasures within them; and perhaps just as important, is that our youth rise into adulthood having learnt to believe they have those beautiful treasures within and can constantly add to them throughout their lives. They need to believe their potential is limited only by their dreams, and anything they can conceive in their mind is achievable. To do this they need devoted adults who not only know how important education is, but also have a sincere interest in youth development and willingly commit their time to be trustworthy role models and counselors.

With so much negativity going on in the public school system, neighborhood difficulties, etc., children must be taught and told and reminded regularly that they are special, capable, have endless potential and that they are loved. This kind of self-esteem and self-respect support is just as crucial to their overall education as math and language. If children feel inadequate and subpar to others, they won't be able to achieve their capabilities.

We live in the Information Age, which is the notion that the availability and the regulation of information is an essential trait of this relatively new era in our human progress. The Internet can provide any kind of information for personal knowledge or research. It's a wide-open world with so much information available to us with the click of a mouse. This availability makes education/teaching more convenient than ever. Given this fact, the role of the mentor or counselor should be easier or more difficult depending on how it is defined.

KEEPING UP

Our world is knowledge-based and requires that people acquire the educational skills to enable them to flourish in the marketplace that is very competitive, as well as understand a world turned super complex. So to keep up and succeed, our young folks require an efficient and effective education to prepare them for life and work. This is a serious venture because an education through high school is the strongest road to achieving their dreams. It has been an ever-increasing fact that most jobs require, at a minimum, a high school diploma. Two-thirds of jobs will eventually require some kind of post-secondary education, going forward.

Many countries in the world have needed to focus on implementing programmes to radically increase graduation numbers. To fail high school or drop out is a sure method to guarantee a life of hardship and loss of our youth's potential.

Several issues are required to ensure a superb education for our children: they need to start their schooling career with excellent early childhood education; be capable of reading at grade level; learn critical thinking and problem-solving skills; pass the college and career readiness standards; and it is increasingly important to become college-ready before they graduate high school.

Caring adults are at the center of every child's progress. Parents and other adults serve as advisers, caretakers and guides who are counted on to provide positive and helpful guidance all through the child's development, from pre-kindergarten through high school and beyond. Studies have shown that when children and teenagers are left to their own devices to figure out how to become successful in school and on into the workforce, they don't have the wherewithal to figure it all out on their own. That's why children have parents. As a consequence, we lose many of our youth when they fall through the cracks. Youths need a network of kind, nurturing people, including extended families, coaches and neighbors. These positive influences in their lives will prove to be significantly advantageous throughout their entire lives.

Caring adults are measured by the good relationships they cultivate between parents and their children, with involvement in school and their communities, and as they guide and mentor the youth towards positive futures and personal strength. Even more, young people desire this special resource – adults who cherish the opportunity to coach and mentor the youth and stick by them, teaching vital lessons that will carry them beyond school and into their careers and future families. The next generation will live in gratitude for the great example given. Youth today live in a chaotic world more and more, and have voiced their need and appreciation for more adults to be involved in their lives.

REFINING YOUR EDUCATION

There are other issues that affect the type of education youth can have. The better our healthcare, coupled with the continued overall health of our youth, directly affects the quality of their education. Studies have shown that children with as much education as they can get live longer and healthier lives than those who receive fewer years in a learning environment. Does education really have such an effect on health? The links tied to education and health are also tied to income and ability as well as to available resources that people have access to in order to live healthy lives in their communities.

It's never simple when talking about the connection between health and education. Bad health is a cause of lack of education and restricted schooling; it is the root of educational setbacks. For instance, young people with asthma experience recurring absences, as well as complications with paying attention in class, problems with vision, hearing, behaviour related to being miserable physically and many more reasons.

There are so many physical and mental conditions that can affect the quality and amount of education that it is very challenging to find solutions. And just as tasking is what happens at home, which can absolutely take a toll on a child to merely be able to concentrate in a classroom setting. If the child is hungry, he can't learn with a rumbling stomach. If she's anxious about her mother's safety, she certainly can't pay attention in class. If his headaches are so bad, he can't focus, etc.

All of these complications, which could keep our youth from accomplishing a wonderful education, often start long before the time to start school. Recent scientific research submits that long-lasting exposure of toddlers and infants to adverse childhood incidents can certainly affect the development of the brain and disrupt the child's immune and endocrine systems, which cause biological changes that will give rise to an upsurge of heart disease as well as other problems later in life.

The connection between health and education is a strong mind and will to produce a good person. A driven mind will produce a driven person. A questioning mind produces a curious person.

Having good health and schooling make a young person want to learn more, want to have more, do more and be more.

Adult habits are usually established when children are drawn to harmful activities such as smoking, drinking alcohol or excessive eating during their teenage years. Obviously, they create a real disadvantage for the rest of their lives, fighting addictions that are sometimes impossible to beat and have lifelong consequences.

Remember the example of drilling for crude oil. Just as it takes a lot of effort to drill for oil, it takes many years of heartfelt commitment to dig deep into the center of a child to affect positive change and success. During the refining process of black gold, it takes different forms that are distinct from its raw state. Likewise, a child takes on different attitudes and needs that are distinct from when the child was born. Yet the potential is there to refine and form every child into a happy adult who is well educated and able to support him or herself and the family, providing not only basic needs but a fine life.

APPRECIATE LESSONS OF FAILURE

Many African youths look forward to succeeding, prospering and making a difference. They are always looking for success stories. As a mentor myself, I ask youths to look for failure stories that they can remedy, from which they can learn. I give you a particular example. I once went to the managing director of a failed bank and sat with him and asked him to tell me why they did not pull through. He is a very brilliant man. He had the best of ideas. He was three to five years ahead of the rest. I asked him why he failed, and I listened to his failure story. I learnt much from that discussion – what mistakes to avoid, what not to do, how to prevent failure in my endeavours.

I don't want to hear your success story only; I want to hear your failure story as well. What would you have done differently? What conditions were there for you to have done differently? Why did you make those decisions? This conversation became my guiding light that told me, 'I can't do this or you can't do that because the person who did that failed'. You have more lessons to learn in failure than lessons from success. If you don't learn these lessons, your business will die.

I used to listen to the teachings of Julius Nyerere, an African leader. In most of his conversations, he discussed more about his failures than his successes. He left his success to be told by those who talk about success. His seeming failures are laced with principles of success.

Sometimes, my mentees ask me to tell them my success story. I respond with I am not sure it is a success story. Nobody will say they are successful until they have finished their tenure. I have had interesting times. Moments filled with interesting challenges, moments of joy and happiness. Even at downtimes, it is difficult for me not to be grateful. But more importantly, my successes have come from the dips in life. It is important to understand the environment that accounts for the decisions taken. The issues that we face as a nation account for certain decisions.

Being a chartered accountant, it has been difficult to find myself as an entrepreneur because I'm almost set in my ways. Accounting disciplines a person in a manner that makes it difficult to do business in a larger sense. So, I have to relearn to be able to read in between the lines doing business in Nigeria and by extension in Africa and outside Africa.

People say I am successful today because they see me revive seemingly impossible organisations that appear to be completely dead and gone. But I have been able to work with people to make those businesses come back to life. If you can convince a set of people to focus on the wins rather than the downsides, it is possible there could be an easy break to a successful venture. When we got to SGBN, we realised that indeed, if you serve the true essence of your story, then people are able to see the painting on the wall and they themselves begin to decorate the painting to what they believe your vision to be.

SGBN had been dying for ten years. My management team and I had many discussions, including how people had lost money. Ten years is a long time — someone who was 56 would now be 66 and ready to retire. Someone who was 45 is 55 and has no job. If you don't have the courage to ask for money no matter how dead the situation is, the chances to succeed are slim. Why do I say people had to have courage to ask for the money they needed? There was already the perception that the bank had failed, and the physical evidence was in front of everybody that this bank had failed. It's not going to rise up suddenly, nothing is going to happen, it's just another failed bank.

The liabilities were hanging out there, accrued interest, regulators were not happy with what had happened, and yet we were saying give us money to pour into this sinking hole. But we understood that there was a greater good beyond the new imminent financial gain that seemed to present itself.

We considered the man who was 60 years old and is now 70 years old and needs that money to take care of himself in his old age. The man who was 30 years old then is now 40 years old and probably has children to pay school for. He needs a loan to survive because of his ever increasing everyday costs of living. To him it feels like the day will never end, the week will never end, the month will never end, the year will never end. The bills are mounting, the family pressure is mounting. And there are businesses in front of him that are growing and there he knows what to do but he can't do it, because his savings are locked up in a bank – Doors Closed!!!

Such a man needs to think and dream hard. A dream that can produce a vision of what is possible. The interpretation and implementation of the vision is more important than the vision. He needed to look for someone to explain what the dream, his vision, was all about. Like ideas, we can dream ten times in a day, but interpreting that dream and then implementing that interpretation into workable, actionable, bits and pieces, minute by minute milestones is the difference between succeeding and not succeeding.

I told this story to my son. I said, 'You always believe that you are ready to go into life, but if you don't stop to think through where you are headed you will never get there. You must know the answers to basic questions such as, how are you going to pay the workers? How do you take your product from where you are to where it needs to be? Who told you your product would be needed, how can you be sure?'

I said BlackBerry was one of the best things that happened to the world, but how long did it last? Ten years. Is it still on the list of the best businesses? No. If you look at the list of the best ten companies ten years ago, and compare it to the ten best on today's list, you would be shocked that not even one is on the ten best companies. Such is the level of turnover and change driven mostly by innovation and policy (environmental factors).

THE WAIT TIME

Most visions and dreams are achieved because the waiting period was not harnessed and/or the vision was not well interpreted. Visions that are not well interpreted give rise to people digging in the wrong farm. For example, whenever you raise an issue that concerns a vision and someone believes you have a vision, they begin to think of all the things they could do with that vision. And they think of all the things that you may not have considered, saying, 'Suppose the road ends only ten kilometres after you start. What if you meet a big mountain after ten kilometres, do you have the tools to tear through the mountain?

Do you have the tools to climb up and over the mountain?' That is an interpretation of a vision. Taking time to answer these types of questions is vital.

Considering beyond the nowness of the value you would create is what the wait period is about. If you invest and allow a wait period beyond two to five years, you just might hit a jackpot.

I can tell you that though we succeeded in changing SGBN to Heritage Bank; and within eighteen months, we jumped into another deal where we acquired Enterprise Bank, in hindsight, I should have waited because that deal set us back ten years, in terms of bank growth projections. It is important to understand that at the point of purchase, we believed we needed Enterprise Bank to survive. What we did not put into consideration was a wait time between when we bid and made a case for it and when we bought it. If we had invested the time to wait and look at life after the acquisition, we would have seen that it was not a good deal for a lot of value was destroyed and we struggled.

Why do I say that? We were a small boutique and unique bank at the start of Heritage bank but we wanted to be a national bank with wider spread, expanding inorganically. We believed we had products with national appeal but were con-strained by our regional distribution channels. We overlooked the all-important 'Wait Time'.

If we have adopted the principle of wait period, we would have known that this venture was not a dash – it is supposed to be a long race. I am talking about bequeathing. We had said our vision was to create, preserve and transfer wealth across generations. To create doesn't necessarily mean to add on; creation is an originality in itself, unique in formation. We completely threw that away and wanted to be like everybody else. We forgot the uniqueness of our vision and went with everybody else. The cost was huge, and we are still paying. The cost you bear for a singular mistake of misinterpretation of vision, not paying attention to your wait period, cannot be quantified in monetary terms. You lose your credibility and essence, then comes the character – your ability to wait and not give up.

One of the difficult things in bouncing back after a season you consider a failure is to admit your mistakes and again reach out with the same relentless pursuit and tenancity to be true to yourself and your vision. You must be able to admit your mistakes. It is easy to blame everybody else for your mistake – but a person of character and integrity will take responsibility and in the long run will be credited with much success.

Although other people may have truly been the reason for the failure of vision, if you nonetheless admit mistakes were made, you can take the bold step backwards. Now, most of the time people say bold steps are taken forward. But if you take a bold step backwards, you will actually be where you should be. This could be even two years back. I heard somebody say if a plane is flying and it encounters a storm, the pilot will turn the plane to avoid it. He doesn't go back to the airport to take off again, he just adjusts the path as it goes along; this is true for the circumstance.

In the business world, you may actually need to go back to the field where you took off. If you do not, you may never find your path. Bold steps backwards are that most difficult place of accepting you're wrong, accepting you have made a mistake and taking in the effect of the mistake. You may wish away some of the effects of the mistake, but this is not going to happen if you want to truly go forward. You need to be true to yourself, you need to be true to your colleagues. They also need to come to the table to know that you as the leader accept your mistake. You take responsibility for the overall misinterpretation of the vision that led to the failure, then you share the responsibility with them if there is still cause to be pursued.

HEALING TIME

After that unsuccessful business venture, I did something that my team probably couldn't believe. I reached out to Dr Sam Adeyemi, founder of DayStar Christian Centre and self-image expert, and said to him, 'My team is hurting. I need you to speak to my team to help them reduce the hurt after a failed business deal'. People underestimate the psychological hurt failure causes in an organisation, and the effect on individual members of the organisation. Failure has an impact on people's health, on their psyche, every-thing about them, even on their courage towards doing business, until they admit the fear and their part in the failure.

Second, although teams have the confidence and believe they can do their jobs better than anybody else and they have the ability to do it, when they hit a rough patch, the brakes are off and the car careens off the road and lands in a ditch. To bring the car out of the ditch, they have to get out of the car and into the mud. They must believe and know that the mud is part of the process of bringing the car out of the ditch. That psychological turn is a very big U-curve, not a V-curve. Those of us who are economists talk about a marginal utility curve. A V-curve means that I broke down but I immediately rose. Facing a mistake and rectifying it means things are not going to rise immediately. There is a plateau at the bottom before you rise. That plateau is another waiting time. So even bouncing back is not a ball hitting a wall. When you run off the road and you get stuck in the mud, the waiting time begins!!

You serve your wait time; and if you do not have the strength of character to serve your time, you must seek help to overcome the hurt psychologically after a failure. I remember days when I didn't want to stand up from my bed. I remember days when I was ashamed to even walk into my office. I remember days when I didn't even want to go to the regulator's office. If I saw a regulator's call, I wanted to hide; but I realised I could bounce back until I faced my colleagues one on one and told them it is well.

You need to help your colleagues to come out of the psychological trauma themselves. It is not just about the job, it touches you psychologically and you must overcome the pain of failure. It's like a ditch, and to get out of it you must endure the mud and mess and effort that comes with it.

Following that, you need to see light at the end of the tunnel; but therein again lies another pitfall. At the point you're coming out, it's easy for every and anything to befall you because you want to quickly come out and breathe. And like they say in the African parlance, a tortoise who has been in a ditch for donkey years when he is to be released tomorrow and he suddenly realises that where he stays stinks (because he's being released tomorrow), starts shouting, 'Please help me out, it's stinking'.

The truth is, you need to wait out your time. Put things in the proper perspective – you won't lose. There are bruises all over you, but they will heal. The ability to stay so you can get healed makes the difference, and you need a lot of help. This is a time when you need to talk to people, you need to talk to your mentors, not necessarily because they are older or have more experience than you, but because they can just be your friends.

The waiting time is also a good place to discover who your friends really are; beautifully so, and the most interesting part of it. There will be those who walk away even before you say anything and those who stay and just watch you with no words. They console you because they know you're hurt; that even in the midst of laughter, you're weeping. Only those who understand will help you through the process of healing.

The building process can be painful, it is indeed a painful process. How does the leader handle pain when everybody around is looking up at you for direction? People have asked me to answer this question, and I don't know how – I wish there was a recipe for a leader to follow. There's none. People ask me,

'How can you afford to smile in the midst of this pain? How can you smile in the midst of seeming betrayals when the ones you need most walk through the door and leave you high and dry? How can you smile?'

It becomes an issue of what is the person's essence, what is their substance. If you focus on the act or the situation, you will lose it. You need to stay in tune with your personal essence. I tell my colleagues, 'You've not stopped being you, you are still you. It's okay to blame yourself for the wrong, but don't stay in a pity party. Pull yourself together and begin to think about what to do. If you want to give yourself a pity party, you will hurt continually and will never heal'.

As a leader, all the focus is on you. If you smile, it is well; if you don't smile, it is not well. You need to take leadership at its essence, not in you the person. *There is a difference between you the person and the essence of leadership.* It is to stop being bossy and be the caring father, the sounding board, the one who everybody blames for the error and absorb all the criticisms without beating yourself to death. Being a good leader is allowing them to put their burden on you so that they're relieved; because when they are relieved, they begin to think of how to make it better and to relieve you of your burden.

My staff come to me saying, 'MD we are with you. We know you are with us and it's going to be well'. You encourage them and they encourage you. If you don't give them the opportunity to encourage you back by encouraging them, you lose your leadership, you lose the essence of leadership. It is not about how good you are but how you understand the problem and the essence you put out. Leadership is an interesting course in life and an interesting phenomenon, interesting philosophy, all put into one.

You do not really know a leader until you face a life-threatening crisis. You must immediately set a goal worth beyond yourself. You look beyond the immediate overall organisation crisis to the individuals who make up the organisation. You focus on the people who have lives to live as they run towards the goal. You think about the child of a junior officer who has no responsibility for the decision he took that caused the deal to fail. How will he pay the child's school fees? You begin to think in terms of their survival, in terms of what you need to do to give them hope to survive.

Once you go to that space, you provide the leadership that is required and you go out of your way to begin to aggregate the responsibilities and then discuss this vital challenge. You must communicate with them. It's most challenging when you sit with your colleagues and tell them, 'I'm sorry I took the wrong turn… but guys, trust me, we are going to come out of it stronger and better'. Like I told my colleagues, 'We are going to buy another bank, and you may choose not to go on this route with me again, but those of you who will stay with me will help me make it happen – and I appreciate you'.

Take Action

The many issues that face us in trying to commit to our children, a quality education, giving them every opportunity to flourish and gain valuable experiences and life lessons, seem daunting and overwhelming at times. But there are small ways that we can implement which will give big results. All it takes is a little effort from each of us to make a big difference in the lives of children who are so dependent on adults who care about them, guide and mentor them so they have a head start to a great life that will serve them well. The following are a few ideas:

➡ Whether new parents, grandparents or just someone who values children, you can make a big difference in the quality of children's education and health by giving a little bit of your time each week at a local school helping children understand subjects difficult for them. Everyone has a stake in every child's education – they are our future.

➡ Monitor your child's television, video game and Internet time. They are all distractions, are addictive and can destroy creativity in children. It's suggested that 'screen time' be limited each day.

➡ Encourage your child to read. It's proven that by reading to your child from infancy on to when they can read to you is the most beneficial activity you can do together. If children learn that reading is fun, it stretches their imagination, and takes them to lands they never knew existed, just by reading good books. Reading gives children a huge advantage and a head start in education. A regularly scheduled trip to the library becomes a worthwhile family outing.

➡ Seek out a failure story and work with yourself or your team on how to take a bold step backwards and rebuild.

➡ Discuss the learning points and build a template for corrective measures.

➡ Create a scenario to enable you to say, 'I am sorry, it was my fault'.

Chapter 7

Thinking and Organising for the Next Generation

THE FUTURE IS HERE

Generational organisations can only be built with a mindset of wealth creation. In our present society, many youths are interested in getting riches. This is the mindset that has been pervading throughout space from time immemorial. This mindset must be eliminated if we are to see progress. As mentioned in a previous chapter, there is no company in Nigeria today that has outlived the generation that created it. This is due to our mindset of a one-man business mentality. In our present

99

model of business and leadership we believe that one man is the owner, and therefore the secretary, treasurer and all other leadership positions. If he goes away, the second generation kills the business because they were not part of the visioning and innerworkings of the company and had little or no training, understanding or mentoring regarding policies, procedures, personnel or even strategic intents of the company.

We must develop a 'can-do-together' long-term mindset and eliminate the can-do-alone and get rich mindset. Wealth is more than financial gain – wealth creation is what we need in Nigeria. Our leadership should know that wealth exists in every part of the country and should seek ways to obtain it and use it for the betterment of all. We can own or buy the assets required in every situation where opportunity arises. We can lease the required asset in place of buying it and save money. We can make agreements that transcend the current generation. We can give the next generation the required mindset; and as we ease out, they will continue the process – then we begin to have generational organisations that improve over the years, benefiting not only the families but communities, regions and the nation.

If we look at the advanced countries today, we see generational corporations like Walmart, Ford, Daimler and Guinness that are in their second or third generations. In advanced countries, owners of organisations work and preserve it for future generations. Until we change our visioning mindset and begin to create enterprises for tomorrow, there is no future to bequeath to the youth. That leadership journey and discussion has to start with the fundamentals in training them. We must begin to train the youth to make better choices. I believe that the worst thing we can hand over to our children is money. Many may disagree and it's okay.

In order to create an environment where business can be developed and thrive, government and citizens must be ready in every way to make it happen, to help with determination so that business will work for the next generation. This preparation must begin in young families by teaching the children and young adults that security for the future means building together, learning together and making commitment together. Raising children with a belief system of family loyalty and security is the key to a successful family business. It can be done. All that's needed is an idea, a dream, optimal thinking, a strong belief system, mutual respect that everyone is part of the family unit — and nothing can keep us down. And that is exactly what the famous Arthur Guinness, the world-renowned brewer, did.

THE GUINNESS STORY

Picture a young man meeting others in a large house of worship in Ireland with his spouse and young children. He lived about the same time as the creation of the founding fathers and was a rising entrepreneur in Dublin. His name is Arthur Guinness, and he was a brewer, and it is difficult to overstate just how vital beer was to the citizens of Dublin in Guinness' day.

Guinness resided in a time when no one understood or even knew about microorganisms and the way illness multiplied. They regularly drank from the exact waters in which they discarded the refuse and human muck. Without knowing, they contaminated the lakes and rivers all around their towns. Folks died as a consequence, and it caused almost everybody in Guinness' day to stop drinking water completely. In its place, they gladly drank distilled brews.

To support and heal their tortuous society, some folks turned to making beer, as the procedure for brewing and the alcohol that came from it killed the bacteria that caused the water to be unhealthy. The brew was healthy in ways that scientists are finally starting to appreciate. Monks made it, evangelicals brewed it and hopeful young entrepreneurs like Arthur Guinness brewed it. And they became valued and privileged for their unique works.

What made this Sunday in Guinness' life so significant was who he was about to hear that day – John Wesley was in town. Wesley was the originator of the Methodist church, the gentleman who began a small assembly at Oxford University from which a significant restoration grew. Wesley and his family desired to be good Christian people – to 'perfect holiness', as they said – and as they preached the Gospel, they gave to the underprivileged and visited inmates and raised funds to serve the indigent.

Entire towns were transformed by the proselytising of John Wesley, his brother Charles and the famed George Whitefield. And now John Wesley had gone to Dublin and was evangelising at the spiraling St. Patrick's Cathedral. And Arthur Guinness was there:

> We do not know exactly what Wesley preached, but we can know a few things. Wesley would have called the congregation at St. Patrick's to God, of course, but he also would have had a special message for men like Guinness. It was something he taught wherever he went. 'Earn all you can. Save all you can. Give all you can', he would have insisted. 'Your wealth is evidence of a calling from God, so use your abundance for the good of mankind'.[1]

Arthur Guinness got the message. He also went to work with a determination of success. Stimulated by Wesley's sermon, Guinness poured himself into establishing the first Sunday school classes in Ireland. He gave huge sums of money to the underprivileged, was involved on the board of a hospital intending to help the indigent and bravely confronted the material indulgences of his own societal class. He was nearly a single army of one in reform.

The Guinness' decided they could make society better by improving the existences of their workers. They began by paying better wages than anyone else in Ireland. And then they thought they would offer an entire schedule of amenities to expand the lives of their workers. With the passing of years, they became some of the most substantial, life-changing workers the world had ever recognised.

If the Arthur Guinness story was only around Arthur Guinness, it would be a minor annotation in the annals of history. However, Arthur Guinness added to all of his decent works by educating his children about the standards he had learnt and lived by. His children, as a result, built the Guinness Corporation on the potency of their father's dreams and faith. This is how the great legacy of the Arthur Guinness generations became the great legacy of the Guinness family.

And that is how family businesses begin, improve and grow into great successes for generations. Guinness involved his whole family by explaining and showing them what a great idea he had because Dublin and eventually Ireland had a problem that needed solving – the water system was filthy and caused disease. Arthur's invention provided a great solution to a big problem. People could stop drinking the contaminated water and instead indulge in the tasty brew Guinness made.

NOTE

1. Elise Hilton, 'World War II, God and Guinness', *Acton Institute Powerblog* (blog), 17 March 2015, https://blog. acton.org/archives/76779-world-war-ii-god-and-guinness. html, accessed 18 June 2020.

Take Action

Arthur Guinness' method and plan for starting a profitable family business is the format to follow. Of course, the business was started when Guinness' children were very young. It takes at least one full generation to learn the ideals and function of an enduring family business. The following are a few tips for implementing your own family profession:

➡ Start thinking early about ideas. Children are never too young to start developing in them an understanding of why a family business is a great idea. It can be profitable for future generations and provide stability.

➡ It's always wise to take some time to decide about the best business in terms of cost, location, marketing and sustainability. How many employees might you need? Will you need specialised help or can anyone learn the business?

➡ Look around closely at your community. Ask around what people see that the community needs or what they would like to see available that isn't yet. The old axiom is very true — find a need and fill it. That was Arthur Guinness' ace in the hole, his brilliance. And it paid off for him and his family for many generations and it's still going.

Chapter 8

GLOBALISATION AND GLOCALISATION

Globalisation has been a popular concept, especially with multi-cultures. Today's leaders have to know how to operate on different levels at various times, build specific institutions and have a high level of experience connecting with the world of today and tomorrow. How can leaders become global in their thinking?

First, it is important to consider a new cultural aspect of globalisation – glocalisation.

Glocalisation is being local with a global perception. It is the local ability to influence, control, empower and develop your system to gain international recognition. You cannot be global without first setting yourself in a local space. Our 'Africanness', for lack of a better word, can't be global until we first understand who we are and express ourselves from a local stance. Each time we try to be what or who we are not, we miss the mark. Anytime we define ourselves in the context of what others do, we miss the mark. *It is the smallest of what we do in our little space that makes us global.*

As people begin to study the reasons behind our success in that small space, we become global. For example, if you attend Harvard Business School and write a case study, they study your success, and then take it global for an international understanding. That is why a Chinese person goes to the US to study, but applies his local languages and ideologies. He is global in his study, but local in its application. If he tries to do the opposite, he will become a stranger in his own hometown. A leader who does not start within his local space and framework to project what is possible, will always miss the mark.

Many people are obsessed with the concept of globalisation and have not taken the time to understand the process. I don't really have a problem with globalisation, but I am concerned with the way Africa and Africans are going about it. We are accepting and importing global standards without first exploring the possibilities of those standards within our context.

That is why businesses and ideas that are working elsewhere fail here. Some attribute it to the soil, and they are not far from the truth. They only lack a better description of the phenomenon. There is nothing wrong in having a global recognition, but we must first have a local recognition. We must succeed at home and in our small spaces and corners first. Only when we do this can the world be interested in how we are succeeding and then attracted to come and learn how we did it.

GLOCALISATION SUCCESS FIRST, GLOBALISATION NEXT

When others take our local successes/principles, and apply them in their own context with similar success, then our local methodology to success gains global recognition or becomes global. This is how the Singaporeans did it. The whole world today is interested in their success story — which is largely local. They started in their locality and achieved success in it first. The world is rushing to Dubai because their leadership looked at what works best for them locally and built on it successfully and have been able to attract global recognition by so doing.

Globalisation is simply glocalisation at a larger or international scale. Africa must learn how to adapt or interpret global forces locally. Importing the former prime minister of Singapore, Lee Kuan Yew, to rule Nigeria does not guarantee success because he would need to understand the context in which to apply what has worked for his people in Singapore to Nigeria. What works in Singapore might not work in Nigeria or any other part of the world simply because the local context was not taken into consideration in the design. In glocalisation, we begin from our local space and give due consideration to the possibilities that are affordable therein for there to be success.

It is very pertinent that in our efforts and attempts to gain global recognition, we must always take into consideration the local context. Now let's look at an extremely successful local company that stepped into the global economy.

MCDONALD'S GOES GLOBAL

A perfect success story and example of glocalisation, is McDonald's, the giant USA fast-food chain. Let's consider what the company did when they took their brand to China and India. McDonald's is a global brand that first achieved local recognition; and in its efforts to achieve global recognition, it had to consider the local context of the countries it intended to reach. The company is mostly known for fast foods; but when the company decided to take their business to China and India, they didn't serve the Chinese burgers and milkshakes, rather they introduced new rice meals that blend with the local Chinese as well as Indian cultures.

If they hadn't taken the food cultures – local context – into consideration, their venture would have been a disaster. They had to localise the content of their product first before it gained acceptance in the Chinese culture. Theirs was a global brand accepted at home and so many other countries; but in trying to further their global reach into China and India, they had to understand the local context of these places first.

Now we look at an example of a large USA company trying to globalise without first educating themselves about local culture – Starbucks, the giant American coffee maker. Starbucks wanted to open a café in the Forbidden City of China in 2007. Despite being successful in other Chinese cities, Starbucks failed in the Forbidden City because of a local negative connotation of 'Western influences' in the Forbidden City, which Starbucks failed to take into consideration. Through a successful web-based campaign, Starbucks was asked to quietly and peacefully close shop in the Forbidden City. If they had recognised this local issue, they wouldn't have wasted their resources.

As a rule of thumb, we must first think local before thinking global! The cultural beliefs of a foreign country are of utmost importance when considering going global. Hurting feelings out of ignorance because the homework wasn't done first won't sit well. Being inconsiderate of social mores, religious beliefs and strong opinions is a sure recipe for failure.

GLOCALISATION

Some of us don't believe in globalisation, we believe in *glocalisation*. You are local with a global perception. You cannot be global without setting yourself in a local space.

A leader who does not start within his local place and space and project what is possible within his framework will always miss the mark. People who think former President Obama could leave the USA and become the president of Nigeria are mistaken – he would not succeed because he knows nothing about Nigeria.

He wouldn't be able to do well because he doesn't understand the system of leadership within the Nigerian context.

We have been studying the Singaporeans and how they succeeded while other countries didn't get it right. We observed that success is contextual and it is situational. Dubai succeeded with plans that were suitable to their own environment, and now the whole world is there to celebrate their glocalisation.

Glocalisation is your local ability to influence, control, empower and develop your local system to have international recognition. I sometimes refer to it as the local leadership playground for international success.

Take Action

The key here is getting leaders on a local level to understand how important it is to the success of a country to make goals, seek the best methods for success and train the younger generation to look ahead, not backwards. Anything that can be conceived in the mind for the betterment of a local society is a worthy project for the long haul. Improvements, new ideas and the effort it takes to put it all together and make it work takes time. Whatever amount of time it takes is worth it. Importantly, it has to start locally.

- ➡ Patience is necessary to teach and impress upon youth that if they are going to effect positive change so society becomes happier, secure and better off financially and otherwise, they must step up and take charge.

➡ It takes a determined and humble leader to begin
a campaign that will bring in the right people
who can influence and encourage people to jump
onboard locally.

➡ To promote a worthy cause locally – in the communities, states, etc. – approach organisations already
established that might want to step up and help
fundraise, talk to government officials for their
support, contact citizens who have the means and
funds to help with fundraising.

Chapter 9

MERGERS AND ACQUISITIONS – OVERCOMING PITFALLS

Mergers and acquisitions are essential topics to discuss in Nigerian companies. Where I focus in this chapter is answering the question: Do acquisitions that lead to mergers create value?

I have been fortunate to be involved in quite a number of acquisition deals. When acquiring a business or asset, the general thought is that it will lead to an increase in the value of the shareholders' net worth. But too often, as we enter into the acquisition process, we realise that a lot of important aspects have not been seriously considered by most organisations. The 'hard issues' of the balance sheet, perceived customer acquisition and perceived asset acquisition looked good. But the 'soft issues' – the ineffective and faulty aspects – are what ultimately lead to acquisition or merger failures.

DEALING WITH 'SOFT ISSUES'

The number one soft issue is culture. Where the cultures of both organisations are not aligned – the chances of a successful merger is very slim. Unless there is a deliberate effort by those driving the acquisition and the merger to focus primarily on the people, the culture of the people and what kind of culture they want to drive in the new entity that emerges, the emerging entity will be unsuccessful and stakeholders will lose a lot of value.

In the past, I have fallen victim to flawed reasoning. I felt that I needed to impress on the people that the organisation we were acquiring had values that could be easily leveraged upon, and that a one-week culture workshop would be enough. I didn't realise that a daily routine such as a boot camp should have been instituted to drive home the desired culture before leveraging in perceived values.

The level of people's competence in the organisations we were acquiring had not been adequately and/or accurately assessed; and because the level of competence was not properly dimensioned, we let go of quality staff with a blanket notion that everybody in a perceived group/level were not good enough. That fallacy of simple statistics cost us much more than we bargained for in terms of value to the organisation and culture alignment.

The result, shareholders' value depreciated by nearly 80 per-cent, causing a near loss of the entire organisation. That is a major lesson for anybody considering merging organisations. Focus on the soft issues, the culture and the people's compe-tence. I'm not sure consultants can give a better idea of how to review the existing resources in terms of personnel, their talents and what is driving those talents. In fact, what we observed was that there are leaders within leaders in the organisation that we acquired, and those leaders were not adequately addressed or even identified. If we had identified them earlier, we would have been able to leverage a better deal.

Here I am saying, it's not enough to say, *'I have a plethora of talents in the organisation we are going to acquire or merge with'*. You need to know what is the driving force — soft issues behind what drives those people. Is it a person? Who is that leader? Not the managing director or the acting general managers, but the opin-ion leaders, leaders that influence the people's thought process, leaders that get them to rise as one and fall as one. When you identify those people, it is important to engage them in a con-structive manner so you can sell your ideas and visions to them. If these leaders buy in, this will make all the difference.

I mistakenly thought that by gathering everybody in a large auditorium and using 35 to 40 minutes to address our vision, that I would sell our story and everyone would be onboard. Little did I know that many of the acquired organisation's staff held resentment towards those who acquired their organisation. There was a level of resentment towards the 'conqueror' that was driving them. A resentment driven by fear... Fear of being looked upon as second best.

Now going forward, I know that there must be a serious conversation. The leader must always have a conversation with all his 'troops'. It's not a list of commands, it's making them see what they achieved and helping them see what more they can achieve while pointing out areas where improvements can be made. Learning from my initial failure, I make it a point to have those conversations in my office with smaller groups of people.

While at it, I asked my direct reports to have the same conversations with their staff so that they can become familiar with and understand the ups and downs of the organisation, the result of which made me stop that process again because there was a 'mythical effect' that emerged projecting that the organisation's leader was somewhere 'out there' and the rest of the team is 1km behind. To have a productive organisation, the leader can't be 'out there' and the organisation lagging behind. When there is such a disconnect, the organisation won't go forward, so I needed to stop and turn back.

I recommend you stop, go back and have those conversations one-on-one. I called this technique 'management by wandering'. I go to managers' offices and allow them to give me feedback. I give them the freedom to tell me what they think. What *they* think drives the organisation, not what I think. Then I ask one or two of them to write down their ideas and suggestions, and I put the write up online on my platform. This gives the person who has written it a sense of my worth and that the idea is worth sharing.

I also encourage productive interaction through 'knowledge sharing sessions'. Management of team members in the banks, share aspects of the organisations once or twice a week and communicate their knowledge, sharing and discussing issues as they relate to the total vision of the organisation.

I do not interfere too much in how they communicate but when the communication is not going the way it should, I give direction, interject, hold informal sessions with them and try to correct the conversation. This is important – because there is no one leadership or methodology. I don't want my organisations to enshrine me, but for my organisation to imbibe whatever valuable advise and suggestions I can offer and let it have a life of its own and live beyond me – that is what leadership is all about.

When I walk into the managing director's office, I should walk out of the office as myself, while whatever I am able to put into the office of the managing director as myself for the organisation should live within that office. And let that be the standard – that whoever walks into that position should be able to carry on effectively. It should not matter if I am there or not, the organisation should continue to produce. If it doesn't survive, then I have not appropriately transferred leadership.

The method of acclimation will determine whether or not the organisation you are bringing onboard will join in your resourcefulness or be against your resourcefulness. This was a good lesson for me to learn. It takes a long time for some people to accept the fact that you acquired the organisation, but did not conquer them.

Some 'conquerors' have used methodologies of practically shoving their core values down the throats of the 'conquered', almost like a jackboot punishment. This tactic creates a repressiveness within what should be a democracy. The result? Anytime they find a means of hurting the system, they will, creating an oppressed mentality within the organisation. Eventually, there will be fights within the organisation and different silos or camps that are working against the vision and are indeed capable of destroying the organisation. Trying to break those camps and silos of discontent can be a major challenge.

When you have organisations within organisations, you see people recommending lesser skilled persons to positions that are available even when they know there are better talents; but because those talents are in another 'camp', they won't be recommended. The organisation is the loser for it. What does a leader do in that respect? It's not to sit and assume that your immediate subordinate or your immediate report will come to you with a balanced description of the issue. Your ability to understand the secrecies or the leanings of each of your immediate subordinates goes a long way to address these very soft issues. Yes, you would probably be discussing culture at the top, but it doesn't positively outlive them, and these are issues to confront and solve.

DEALING WITH MERGED PARTNERS

The next issue when examining acquisitions or mergers involves the external forces where the engagement of the acquiree becomes coloured by what their significant others, their business partners, feel about the merger. Most times we don't consider them, but they usually give warnings, making statements like – 'We don't know why you are merging', or 'You are creating a new vision and not everybody is willing to buy in', or 'The vision that is being created has to start in the evolution', etc.

I have always asked this important question: Does everybody within the system understand who and what the new organisation is? Do they know what the core values of the new organisation are? You may know what it is in the legal terms of agreement, but you need to again resolve and re-evaluate what personal benefits are to be gained by those involved. They need to know the answer to, 'Who am I in this new organisation?' That conversation of who am I must be held from the lowest levels up to the top of the hierarchy. Not only do you have the who am I question to resolve, you also have to answer, 'What new things will happen that would make the mission, as created by the core values, become relevant to everybody on the platform?'

At this point, a vision statement becomes important to the extent that you have to relate the vision to the mission statement and to the core values, and have a kind of deep engagement with almost every segment of the organisation.

The chances of a merger failing due to inadequate appreciation of the soft issues is 90 percent, but if you deal with and solve the soft issues and somebody asks if you did your due diligence, you can confidently answer, 'Yes I did', knowing success is for real.

Unfortunately, there are usually certain relationships and/or bodies that are buried and are not on the negotiating table, and they don't show up on the balance sheet. But upon merging they appear and crystallise not only in court cases, but also in disagreements.

I was involved in the Heritage Bank and Enterprise Bank merger. The management team and I suddenly woke up one morning and found out that there were more than 12,000 cases in court involving the organisation. With that many cases in court, how would we manage? Some of the cases had been in court for years on end. Our eyes were not on that board and suddenly we were faced with all those issues, which involved relationships with people we didn't even know.

We didn't even look at this side of the bargain during the merger, so we ended up having liabilities that materialised and had to be dealt with. Some of those cases were resolvable within minutes with relationship officers. But it took reality hitting us head-on to see a wobbly organisation and realise that soft issues must be dealt with quickly and effectively.

In mergers and acquisitions, you must, of course, understand the material value of what is on the table, your vision must be clear and you need to earn market shares — but the soft issues are the most critical for the survival of any business development.

VISION AND ENTERPRISE

All my life, I have been in private enterprise. I have been asked to share or lead conversations that deal with vision and enterprise. If I had a crystal ball, I would say vision is what every one of us should aspire to have. As mentioned before, unfortunately, vision is nothing. I have been in this visioning business. I had three solid years of attending Harvard Business School, learning theories that started hundreds of years ago that rely on vision. They taught us conventional principles. Vision, mission, core values mean you have an organisation. We wake up to write the vision and the mission, but we forget the core values.

In my opinion, vision has to be connected to a human being. In the absence of the human being, vision is nothing. It starts with you, the person. No matter how well educated you are, in the absence of you being present there can be no vision. That presence transcends the sovereignty of a nation. That presence is in the human self.

What's the purpose of life? What's your purpose? What do you seek to achieve as a person? You must keep asking these questions. You should if you want to make a difference as a leader. This is the true birth place of a successful enterprise.

THE PILLARS OF VIRTUOUS ENTREPRENEURSHIP

Certain things don't change, no matter how you look at them. The first thing is the human element. Every business has its human element, its own soul. You need to appreciate the soul of the business. I say to people who ask, 'Banking is not a business. Banking is a service'. As an example, Heritage Bank is a service company in the business of banking. Until you define who you are, you will not understand who you are or what you can do. For any business to succeed, the first thing to find out is who you are; if you cannot define who you are, you can't set what you can do.

You can't say, 'I am a Nigerian and receive benefits in Britain'. The only way you can receive benefits from Britain is if you identify yourself as British. The question then becomes, who is a British person. Your identity is your vision, your core values and what defines you.

If you can't define what is your vision, you can't articulate what your vision is. You need vision. You need purpose, and you need core values. In business school, they teach you to determine your vision first, then the mission and then core values. But to me, that is turning the order on its head. I would rather propose the following order: your core values define you; the mission is what you can do; then go ahead and dream, which is your vision. Most people would rather create a vision, define a mission and then come up with core values.

I have always gone against the world's 'best practices' to the extent I can prove over and over again why they are wrong. Why am I saying this? The classic theory is to have a vision, have a mission and then create core values. But to me that is like saying: To build a house, find the building contractor first, determine the materials next, then find the architect to design the building. The house is the vision. Once you see the vision, the next question is who designs and builds it.

The who is very important. What are his core values, what makes him dream? Why is he dreaming? The "who" is a personality. The definition of the dreaming entity is the core values.

That's why you can say my company has a personality of integrity, strength, service and intelligence. It is important to first *become* before *doing*; if you don't become, you cannot do. We take certain actions for granted, like incorporating a company; the law says the incorporated company has a life of its own, is a citizen of its own. You give the company a name. What you are doing essentially is making the company become before it 'can do'. Most times we create before we become. This negates the natural process.

It is after we are done creating, that we say, okay let's go and fashion a vision for the company. What are the company's core values? Before you name the company, it has to be, it is the process that guides your business. Any other theme is an add-on; in the midst of that circle is the human element who names, who creates and who drives a vision. So, naturally for me the next after the core values is mission, and vision would follow based on the personality defined and/or desired.

The most important element of the organisation is the human capital, which I have always hoped we will be able to put on the balance sheet some day. If you get your human capital resource right, you can always succeed in business. It doesn't matter what is the business technology that you have, if you don't have the human resource right, you will never succeed in business no matter how well you plan. It is surprising that despite all the development achieved in management sciences, we have not been able to show this most important organisational resource on balance sheets with values attached.

Just like you must define the personality of the company, you must stick to the rules that govern business. If you break the rules, your company will be destroyed. For example, if somebody runs the 100 metre dash and wins without following the rules, disqualification is certain. A modern-day example is Ben Johnson whose name was struck off the medal list because he tested positive for a banned substance in his system. I believe his lack of values caused his problem. Did he train very hard to run that fast? Yes he did, but he did not follow the rules of the game. So, contests must be conducted within set boundaries; anything outside those boundaries is cheating. The business world is no different.

Take Action

➡ Acquisitions and mergers can be handled well if soft issues are dealt with quickly. Think of a recent soft issue that turned into a major problem. Did you deal with it quickly enough?

➡ It takes a determined and humble leader to begin a campaign that will bring in the right people who can influence and encourage others to jump onboard. Do you have the right people in place? Assess your staff and make that determination.

➡ There are always clichés or small groups in all organisations; if they are not aligned with the overall vision of the company, handling these sub-organisations or silos will protect the organisation from being sabotaged. What steps can you take today, if necessary, to either reconcile or eliminate disruptive groups and/or silos?

Chapter 10

CORE VALUES, MISSION AND VISION – GETTING IT RIGHT

The greatest role of a leader is to transfer the vision
of the organisation to the members of the team.

Transferring the organisational vision is important, and must be considered seriously. Do not transfer the vision to one person or a small group of persons in the organisation. If you transfer it to one person, the person may create for himself the post of 'custodian of the vision' and everybody will have to go to the person. What you have done at that point is to create a monster.

If you share it with a larger number of people, the tendency of a greater number agreeing to drive the vision is higher. It would be nice to create a vision structure that is not too rigid. If you create a vision that is circular, which I call an 'Olympic ring', there will be continuous interactions between people who understand the vision, and how it fits into their own expectations and your expectations and someone else's expectations and so on. There is no end in that interaction, which is what the Olympic ring actually represents — a continuous circle of engagement and learning.

For example, if you ask me to draw an organogram, an organisational chart, any day, anytime, I would probably be drawing an Olympic ring. The known formal structures of organisation don't work, they actually create silos in institutions because some people misinterpret the vision and others do not understand the vision at all.

VISION OWNERSHIP

I am a believer in generating a sense of 'ownership'. Leaders have to, as a matter of necessity, get their team members to own the organisation's vision. If there is no collective ownership of vision, organisations will face serious problems. Leaders should aspire to ensure the generational transfer of wealth; wealth in a broader definition not just money — knowledge, values, competence and skills. The leader must understand that before embarking on the process of transferring the vision, he must have the capacity to manage himself first, then decide how to duplicate himself into many.

When the leader gives his direct reports a message for all the team members he needs to ensure that the message is passed along. Sometimes people close to the leader hold back communication. These are the people who create the silos and the kingdoms within the organisation. A leader needs to identify those people who are preventing a cohesiveness within the organisation either to relieve them or ask for a change of attitude. A leader must determine who has what kingdom and have the courage to break it, have the courage to have conversations, deep conversations, very uncomfortable conversations. The reason for such silos or kingdoms within the organisation can easily be traced to ego issues.

If leaders don't discuss these problems directly with the persons involved, the problems could only get more intense and cause the organisation to derail from its set goals/objectives. Leaders have to tackle ego issues head-on, especially if the person tends to gossip, self-praise, manipulate others, wants others to adhere to their own point of view, will not balance arguments or discuss issues. It takes effort to break those kinds of self-aggrandising egos.

A leader needs to have a clear understanding of what an overrated ego can do to the organisation, and he needs to have two or three people who are critical advisers—people who have the interests of the organisation at heart and can be objective. There are no set rules about how to break an egotistical person's mindset, but it must include interaction, frankness, calling people to account, being able to sit with them and hold very difficult conversations.

At a point in time in Heritage bank, we had a difficult matter where we were trying to achieve a balance between two products in the organisation. One group head felt strongly about the way the structure should be and another group head felt otherwise. They had contrary views; thus, I switched the group leaders so that each one would be leading the opposite structure. They each advocated. The moment I switched them, they suddenly became advocates for the way they had previously opposed. Their ego, their personal survival and success, superseded the organisational success. It became clear that personal integrity was not part of the mindset of either leader.

They were both thinking, 'Whichever team you give to me to lead, I have to succeed with them, even if it means doing something wrong or changing whatever methodology I would apply, or if I need to pack up all the staff I have here and go across to the other structure so I can succeed with them, irrespective of what the organisation needs to win!' Ego got in the way of progress. They were mapping existing customer accounts to their loyal team members to the detriment of the overall set objectives of the growing customer base.

This type of issue will confront you as a leader. Some leaders in your organisation or your subordinates want to be successful even to the detriment of another department or another side of the business. They forget that it's one organisation with one vision. You as a leader must then insist that they commit to the overall vision and stop allowing their egos to rule.

My uncle used to cite a disagreeable behaviour of a cousin. He said that the particular cousin of mine had gotten so crooked that if he tried to stretch him, he would break. When some habits, occasioned by ego, are formed and you try to straighten it, it breaks; and when it breaks, the organisation breaks.

As a leader, you need to manage around the known ego, which is crooked, instead of trying to straighten it out, which could break the organisation. The means of managing around it could be a combination of cohesion, negotiation and out right excuse from the organisation. If you find yourself at a discussion table with your team members in negotiation and you cannot be authoritative at that point, try to find a balance; because if you don't achieve balance, you will lose the organisation. Find out who is leading the small group, silo or chiefdom that has been created within the organisation, and then determine how to manage them.

I have over tears observed that the root cause of such ego driven behaviour is deep seated in unresolved soft issues at the beginning of the organisation or visioning process.

A WORD ON PHILANTHROPY

Philanthropy is mostly seen as handouts, which is okay because we need to help the less privileged in our society. My Bible says that we need to reach out to the poor within our communities, which is even a means of blessing to us. But it's important that the rich operate within the same boundaries and compete favourably to enable philanthropy to triumph or to thrive successfully into social responsibility. The target should be to create a better and all inclusive society. Assisting to reduce the gap between the rich and the poor.

As a leader, I have heard people say, you need to give handouts just because you're a leader. But that is not true. Handing out whatever you have as a philanthropic gesture to the next generation or to those you think are poor should be in terms of bettering their lot. Let me use this as an example. A man named MKO Abiola was a Nigerian Yoruba and a successful businessman, publisher, politician and aristocrat of the Egba clan. He handed out as much as he could. What became of his dynasty? Today there are no more Abiola Farms. There is no Concord Group of Companies. There is no Concord newspaper. Is that the example of philanthropy in leadership? The answer is no.

Engage in philanthropy that not only enhances your business but will keep your business growing. Keep it as a corporate social responsibility where it makes money for you and it's simply beneficial to many in society. It is not enough to give people foodstuff to fill their stomach; that is important but if you can educate the youth in various fields of study, craft and trade, thereby giving them a sustainable livelihood for the good of society, then you are helping society. There lies the true philanthropy.

If there are people with handicaps, if I can help them build tables, build chairs, they're better off. To me, enhancing human capacity is what philanthropy is. You have to deal with it in that context when leadership is involved. Philanthropy is not giving handouts to people. If we continue like that, we don't help the poor by giving them money; there's no two ways about it. We need capitalism, we need business to grow as leaders – to be philanthropic leaders. And you must stay in that space of continually growing your business.

And let me also say this, maybe it's not a leadership point but it's something to cast your mind into. Many people whose children are rich, who look down on the downtrodden and just give them handouts, end up having their children being the next generation of those poor people. And the children who are poor, who are downtrodden, work so hard to climb the ladder of success with vigour so that tomorrow they become the rich. As a leader, you need to understand that situations, as those who need aid today, may not necessarily need aid tomorrow. You need to identify them and put them to work so that they become the leaders of tomorrow like yourself.

Take Action

➡ Always identify the egos floating in your organisation. When they have been identified, develop a plan to deal with any disruptions that may arise.

➡ Keep track of your own ego and have others who can truthfully evaluate it, discuss with you the remedial steps to take. Take time each day to review your motivations; have you made any decisions from an egotistical attitude?

➡ Ensure all leaders within the organisation understand that everyone is on the same team, no matter the department. How can you best establish and maintain this vital unifying fact?

Chapter 11

UNLOCKING LEADERSHIP OPPORTUNITIES IN AFRICA

There are many issues in leadership according to Julius Caesar. How can we bring his leadership style into today's world of businesses, especially in Africa? As mentioned in a previous chapter, Julius Caesar was a great Roman military general who later became a ruler. Physically he was weak, which is the fascinating thing about him – his ability to transcend his physical disability and health in order to rise to rule Rome, stamping his name for centuries as one who bore the title of leadership.

Men die for what they believe in truly, but it doesn't mean they don't face adversities. Successful leadership is a marriage of courage and willpower beyond your physical self. For me, everything I say or observe I seek a reference in the Bible to let me know that it's true and simple. For example, I have tried to understand the concept of the lamb and the lion, a lamb being a lion is almost difficult, but in this I saw the lamb is the physical feeling, casual, almost unknowing itself – and the courage is the lion lying within the physical self.

Jesus is referred to as the Lion of the tribe of Judah, yet He is the Lamb of God. You see the quality of human frailty as well as the boldness and strength for which He is known. His essence is that God owns everything so He must be bold as a lion; but in His interaction, He is still a lamb, and that makes us come close to God. These are my personal thoughts. If you have no faith, for you there is no good, there is no bad and your engagement is neither here nor there. So, I want to stress the fact that your faith has a deep influence on your relationship with people and with things directly influencing your leadership style and attitude.

Some people feel comfortable making sure that others are miserable so that they can emerge as leaders. Others are willing to give everything to ensure the best for the people they rule over. I give credit to Nigeria's last president, Goodluck Ebele Jonathan, who said, 'My being president is not worth any human blood'. Only his faith in the sanctity of life could drive him to make that statement. When people don't believe that a human life is worth anything, then everything goes.

In my opinion, faith is critical to leadership; and we may wish to say that law is humanitarian, but law is of faith. That is why we keep saying equity; that if you want equity you should come with a clean hand. What is a clean hand? Faith has to define good. When faith defines good we can know what is bad. In my view, bad can only be defined as the absence of good.

I have already mentioned risk takers and entrepreneurs, but I'd like to expand on that topic and also say that some people think that just because someone takes risks they are leaders. The question is, is a leader the owner of the risk? And more often than not, a leader is not necessarily an entrepreneur.

There are *entrepreneurs* and there are *intrapreneurs*. I can envision a scenario, but my partners would be the ones, the entrepreneurs, to develop it. Having seen what I saw, they become the leaders selling the vision to a wider audience in order to achieve. And in their assessment, they would only bring to the forefront what they want me to decide on, but that decision they bring forward is the risk they are also taking. They must decide for me to decide — and that point of decision making is critical. In entrepreneurial parlance, it is better to take a decision and be wrong than not to take one at all.

LEADERSHIP AND FOLLOWERSHIP

The difference between nations that are failing and nations that are succeeding, in a nutshell, is leadership. But it's not as simple as that, it's caused by the continuous progression of continuously failed leadership, occasioned by failing followership. Leadership is a function of followership. If the followership does not demand the required control boundaries for the leadership, leadership will fail. And as leadership fails, followership fails. As followership fails, countries begin to fail. You cannot bequeath what you have without putting together or cherishing or building. You bequeath what you have built up. If you build up lousy leadership, you bequeath that to the next generation.

If you want them to import from other climes, there can be no other clime structures that will be fit for purpose for your own country, state or community. It has to be based on your cultures, values, traditions and whatnot. We have many failed states in Africa, not because they could have failed from the beginning, but because they jettisoned those things that held them together and went on to look at another man's culture, which was not suited in the first place for their own society.

When talking about leadership, there are interrelated variables that must be considered in the conversation. Poverty starts with the mind. Lack of social amenities starts with the mind. People taking structures and cultural behaviour from communities where there is leadership with thoroughness into their communities, without developing the underlying principles necessary, will show average performance and results. Today, it's not rocket science that Nigerian students are the highest set of graduates of the diaspora. Why are they so? Because from their background as cultural heritage, learning is core to their existence.

They have that entrepreneurial spirit of learning and reaching for the skies. They want to compete to be all they want to be.

Africa is the most underrated, vilified and least understood continent. Textbooks didn't help matters; because after our forefathers in the Egyptian territories showed the world to use people as slaves to build an economy, they exported it to the other world. They thought Africa, in fact, Egypt was a dark place, dark to the extent our colour is dark, our mangrove forests are dark, our woods are dark, our soil is dark. But our blood is still red, and the average European or American sees us as inferior people. So, even when you sell the story of an African greatness, astuteness, trustworthiness and industrious entrepreneurship – the story is taken with a pinch of salt – more like an ancient fairytale.

When they come over to visit – which is always the difficult thing to do in order to win them over to come to Africa – to see for themselves, they see that there are growth margins way beyond what they can even think or imagine. If an American has a 3 percent growth, he is celebrated. When we have a 12 percent growth, we are told it does not cover the country's risk: 'What are you doing with 12 percent? You can do 25 percent'. Because the opportunities are here at the last frontiers in terms of investment, you need to be more convincing.

The truth is that our leadership, African leadership, still goes cap in hand, begging for aid. Africa does not need aid. Africa needs an equal partnership of investment, long-term investment. My challenge is that because the developed economies have the capital, we should be willing to allow them to benefit from the fruits of that capital and improve the ease of doing business in our various countries. This will enable our growth capacity. Local capacity will ultimately overtake the investment and we will be better off long term.

In Nigeria, we'll probably just be dealing with oil, but we have 90 other viable mineral products that we can invest in. Still, nobody is willing to put up capital because even our government is afraid of foreigners coming to invest, thinking that we will lose our resources. We won't. Let them come and invest; and based on their investment, there will be capacity building. When they bring that capacity, we will be able to build and grow beyond the initial threshold.

I call it crossing the chasm. It takes a long time for Europeans or Americans to cross the African chasm. Chasm is that space, almost like a gutter where somebody believes you to a point, and then he stops. For you to grow, he needs to cross the 'African' chasm and there is no bridge except faith and belief. Your work as an investment adviser is to create that bridge for him to walk across with success. Sometimes, the government is supposed to be that bridge. I call it crossing the chasm. The day you can make your partners in the other parts of the world cross the chasm, the trajectory is only upwards.

Only losers do not invest in the next set of leaders, and these are the worst enemies of society or the country. 'When I was young, I was too young to lead. No sooner, I will be too old to lead. I call my generation, the endangered generation'. If this holds true of any society, it will be a sad commentary.

In my early school years, I grew up to see Olusegun Obasanjo as military head of state, and he was only 39 years old. He was entrusted with people resources, and he managed them well. People think that anyone younger than 40 is not fit to lead our country. We find out the 20 and 30-year-olds are now much wiser than even 40-year-olds.

Nigeria has a whole generation of leaders who never had the opportunity to lead the country. The distance between the grand-fathers and fathers of the leaders-to-be of tomorrow is so wide that there's no meaningful leadership impact, because there was no deliberate investment in their leadership development.

The current set of youths, young men and women, are building their leadership skills from telecommunications, from social media groups, from amongst themselves, from peers outside the country, not within. When we tell our young people to go to the village, they say, 'Go to the village? There's nothing there for me to do'. But therein lies our culture, therein lies where we have respect for the elders, where we know that working hard is a key ingredient. Where we know that character is key. Where we know that tenacity is key to leadership. So we have lost a whole generation of wealth. If they are to be the next set of leaders, the time to invest in their leadership skills is *now:* beginning with learning their true Heritage.

It's not an option – it's the only thing to do; and if we don't do it, we just set ourselves up for another failure, as a failed state. When you see any failed African states, check if the leader has been in office there for 50 years, 40 years, 30 years.

The generation next to them knew nothing but that same leader and that leadership is not one you can bequeath to future generations down the line.

Check what the leadership of a country like Rwanda has been. That country came out of a crisis, which is why I say, you only know a leader when there is a crisis. Paul Kagame came to be president out of a crisis – when a million people were murdered because of ethnic 'cleansing' under poor leadership. Kagame turned that around, using the pain of genocide as a threshold for lectures and for lessons. A young crop of leaders is springing up who are being put into strategic areas and are beginning to imbibe a new method, a new culture – alongside the core leadership at the top.

Giving these relatively young leaders responsibilities while the current set of experienced leaders gives guidance provides positive growth outlook on the African continent – and their long-term stories will be different. Today, less than ten years after the crisis, Rwanda and other forward-thinking countries are the destinations for conferences in the African region. How could that be? It can only be with the backing of leadership and succession planning. If you don't plan to succeed, it means that you're set up for failure – simple and short.

To unlock leadership opportunities in Africa, first invest in yourself, to dream big and envision the risks necessary to open heart and mind to life beyond what you are living today.

Take Action

→ Make an inventory of your leadership skills. Decide what are your strengths and write how they can work to your advantage when seeking opportunities. Evaluate also your weaknesses as a leader and appreciate how they can affect others.

→ Think about those who lead around you and with you and evaluate whether they value the sanctity of life, or if they have an 'anything goes' style of leadership for power and ego. What is your leadership style?

Chapter 12

Entrepreneurship in Africa

In his classic book, *Start Small, Finish Big,* Fred DeLuca, cofounder and CEO of the SUBWAY restaurant chain, writes about the importance of entrepreneurs in the growth and development of any nation. DeLuca draws on his own experience and that of twenty-two other entrepreneurs who started on a shoestring budget, shedding light on how they transformed fledging start-ups into industry giants.

Heritage Bank sponsors the television show, *The Next Titan,* which is a reality show that has been designed to take viewers through practical steps on how visionaries can become millionaires. With great insights and street-smart advice, you can personalise each step and make it your own. When watching *The Next Titan,* you will

- discover how and where winners get their ideas and where to look for yours,

- learn ways to increase profitability,

- realise the importance of constantly improving a business,

- know the one thing you must never let happen to your start-up,

- learn the essential lessons of being relentless,

- realise why you should jump in now and fine-tune later and

- gather proven, in-the-trenches guidelines and tools that you can put to work today!

The theme of the fifth season in the series of *The Next Titan* is 'Brains, Charisma & Audacity'.

So, let us start by asking the question: Who is an entrepreneur?

Investopedia describes an entrepreneur as, 'An individual who creates a new business, bearing most of the risks and enjoying most of the rewards. The entrepreneur is commonly seen as an innovator, a source of new ideas, goods, services, and business/ or procedures'.[1] Whereas, according to *Entrepreneur Post* an 'a person who organizes and operates a business or businesses'.[2]

In my own definition, an entrepreneur is an individual who is able to identify and turn practical problems into opportunities for wealth creation and transfer. An entrepreneur drives and is not driven by others. He or she is in charge and makes crucial decisions, he is the one people look to when in need of leadership and is someone who pushes people forward and inspires them.

The entrepreneur has the ultimate responsibility for the destiny of his venture, which can be a company, a project or any other endeavour. This characteristic is vital in any economy and environment. These are the kinds of people who can envision the hardships to come and give people a solution.

THE EVOLUTION OF AFRICA'S ENTREPRENEURSHIP

Now we will briefly look at the evolution of entrepreneurship in Africa in four broad phases: pre-colonisation, colonisation, post-colonisation, and present day.

Before colonisation, entrepreneurship was the order of the day in Africa. Our forefathers were majorly either farmers or craftsmen, building their business enterprises with their skill and physical strength.

At colonisation, while entrepreneurship still thrived, our forefathers became drawn to the ways of the colonial masters and gradually began to embrace Western modernisation and culture. This trend became more prevalent during post-colonisation as those with white collar jobs were seen as society's elite. Little wonder most of us grew up desiring to be doctors, lawyers or professionals in other fields and deserted the trades of our ancestors.

However, as the population size grew, so did the struggle for available jobs, leading to a high rate of unemployment among the younger generation and forcing youths to look inward for income-generating skills.

Today, entrepreneurship is seen as one of the most sustainable job creation tools in Africa, evolving beyond being just skills used as a means of generating personal income. Entrepreneurship has transcended its original meaning to become the following:

- new avenues to create fresh job opportunities,

- skill sets used for refining raw materials into finished products,

- novel and refined ways to deliver basic services,

- channels for economic development,

- mediums to connect to the world and

- sources of self-actualisation and fulfilment.

Raphael Obonyo wrote in a UN-related publication:

With a majority of African nations diversifying from traditional sources of income, entrepreneurship is increasingly seen as a key to economic growth. So far, entrepreneurship has yielded huge returns for entrepreneurs, and according to experts, there lies great untapped potential to drive the African continent into its next phase of development.[3]

KEY ENTREPRENEUR QUALITIES

An entrepreneur must be

1. open-minded,

2. passionate about whatever he/she does,

3. constantly flowing with ideas,

4. creative and always ready to take calculated and/or informed risks,

5. disciplined and confident,

6. an opportunist, a relentless pursuer of opportunities and

7. a problem identifier and solver.

DOES AFRICA NEED A NEW BREED OF ENTREPRENEURS?

Despite its vast wealth of human and natural resources, Africa remains the poorest continent in the world as it is reputed for having the largest number of poor countries among the rest.

A myth is told about the creation of the world; when God created the continents, He bequeathed the West with natural disasters such as earthquakes, hurricanes, wildfires, extreme cold weather, snow and the likes. When He created Africa, He bequeathed it with natural resources ranging from beautiful weather to lush gardens and forests, wild game, crude oil, solid minerals and the likes. A protest ensued from among the Westerners, citing discrimination on God's part in favour of Africa. They wondered why God had blessed Africa with so many resources, while the West had to grapple with little or no resources and harsh weather conditions. God reacted by saying, 'Wait until you see the kind of people I will put in it'.

As of today, most goods brought into the African market are from China — the fastest growing economy in the world — denying our youths job opportunities in manufacturing and other lucrative sectors of economies. Narrowing down to Nigeria, it is evident that we are continually confronted by a wide range of development challenges.

According to the National Bureau of Statistics (NBS), Nigeria's unemployment is at a staggering rate of 23.1 percent, under-employment of 21.2 percent, while youth unemployment-underemployment is gnawing at 52.65 percent.

Indices	From (Q3 2017)	To (Q3 2018)
Unemployment Rate	18.8%	23.1%
Unemployed (within the labour force)	15.9 million	20.9 million
Underemployed (within the labour force)	18.0 million	18.2 million

This worrisome fact does not only have a significant effect on the psyche of the individuals concerned, but also has a destabilising impact on the wider society.

Despite the fully untapped potential in agriculture, Information Communication Technology (ICT) and the service industries, amongst others, promising youths are eagerly seeking means to relocate to other foreign countries in pursuit of 'a better life'. The challenges in our society have created major gaps, and we need a new breed of entrepreneurs in diverse fields who will take up the challenge to create new solutions that will bring about

- job opportunities,

- increase in Gross Domestic Product (GDP) and Per Capita Income,

- development of small and medium-sized enterprises,

- wealth creation and distribution,

- improvement in living standards and

- creation of a more vibrant civil society, contributing to the political stability and placing the African continent on the global front.

WHY IS HERITAGE BANK AT THE FOREFRONT?

According to Evans Wadongo, listed by *Forbes Africa* as one of the most promising young African entrepreneurs, 'Many African governments have not been keen on developing policies that would avert unemployment among youths in a big way'.

While we acknowledge that government and private sector support have recently begun to gain momentum in this regard, we believe that a lot still needs to be done. Africa is filled with young, vibrant and innovative minds capable of becoming world-renowned entrepreneurs of the future. However, this cannot be achieved if we do not support and nurture their idea to become reality.

Heritage Bank is built on the premise of creation, preservation and transfer of wealth from one generation to the next. We believe in the future and believe that the preservation of wealth for the future starts today, hence our unwavering commitment to contributing our quota to building the next 'African Titans' capable of transferring wealth across generations.

STRATEGY

People have said strategy is the be-all and end-all in business. I don't disagree. There is a book that I had tried to help someone write; I didn't write it, I only helped the author put some things in it. I said to the writer, 'Strategy is good; a strategy is like an architect designing a building. If he drops the drawing on the table, it will remain a strategy or design on the table for life. A strategy that has no life in it is of no value. The only strategy that is worth discussing involves the human element. Any strategy that does not have the human element in it is not a strategy'. So the question then becomes, what is more important, the human being or the strategy? I think both are important, but the most important is the human being. Why do I say so?

When I think of the best way to achieve a goal and I document the best way to achieve it, if I don't share it and work towards it, it doesn't exist. But when I share it with a number of people so we can create the means to attain the set goal, that is when strategy is strategy. So, a strategic intent or write-up, for me, has no meaning. But a strategy with an actionable plan becomes the life and the blood of a business. If you don't have a strategy to execute, then you have nothing.

There is the strategy and there is execution; in-between strategy and execution is the most important element – the human being. Just like I said about vision, it is the person that interprets a strategy and then executes it and makes it come alive to the business benefits. Some of us have wonderful strategic documents and strategic intents but we observe no changes. Why? Because the human being, the essence, the reason for the strategy is not in the middle of it. You need the human being to breathe life and meaning into the strategy. Then, changes begin to happen; and results are achieved.

No matter what else people say about strategy in business, it is a philosophy, a concept, it is important, it's what the business needs, it's asking how business can be done better and how can my business be better than others in a competitive environment, all things being equal. Will things ever be equal? The best strategy on the table written out as a document with no execution plan, is as good as not having a strategy at all.

The philosophy and the theory of strategy is very important to business, it comes first, leading the way to execution. Let's say vision is synonymous with strategy. As with an unexecuted strategy, a vision not executed is just a dream. You woke up, you took a walk and you think, it's just a dream. You can dream that you walked on the sea. But if you really want to know whether you walked on water, walk out to the river, a gutter or swimming pool and try to walk across. If you sink, then you realise that what you dreamt about is not possible. You need to redream.

That is why your strategy continually needs to be tweaked, or modified. Tweak your strategy every day if need be. I tell anyone, whoever prepares a business plan – which is a strategy document – when you put the last full stop, the last period at the end of the last sentence, one minute after that everything in that document is obsolete. Because as you are writing it, there could be a policy change or the person you have in mind to execute it might leave or the money you plan for might not be available or the operating conditions may have changed. So, wherein lies certainty? There is no certainty in business, mobile, dynamic homeostasis – it is a relatively stable state of equilibrium between different but interdependent elements or groups. Why? There's a parasympathetic-type rebound. There's always a moving equilibrium. That's why in economics we say we don't have one fixed equilibrium – there're various equilibrium points given the different situations or circumstances.

No matter what happens, you have to find an equilibrium over circumstances that keep changing. As you finish implementing your strategy, your opponent or competitor will execute theirs, and as they finish, you need to have your next strategy ready to execute in order to counter theirs. It's execution of strategy that gives meaning to business, not strategy itself. Strategy in itself is dormant, lifeless, just a piece of paper on the table or an idea in your head. It's the execution that leads to business revolution, business emergence, new idea deliveries and much more.

CONCLUSION

In conclusion, I urge all the participants in this program, especially the sixteen finalists who will emerge in this screening to focus not only on the prize but on the learnings that will happen during your ten-week stay in the house.

Be yourselves, enjoy yourselves – but above all, put in your best in the discovery of your latent potentials as you embark on this exciting journey of becoming *The Next Titan.*

Enjoy

NOTES

1. Adam Hayes, ' Entrepreneur', *Investopedia,* updated 1 July 2020, https://www.investopedia.com/terms/e/entrepreneur.asp, accessed 18 June 2020.

2. Abdallah Alaili, 'What Is An Entrepreneur?' *Entrepreneur Post* (blog), 4 March 2015, https://www.entrepreneurpost.com/2015/03/04/what-is-an-entrepreneur/, accessed 30 August 2020.

3. Raphael Obonyo, 'Africa looks to its entrepreneurs', *Africa Renewal,* April 2016; https://www.un.org/africarenewal/magazine/april-2016/africa-looks-its-entrepreneurs, accessed 18 June 2020.

Appendix

Converting Your Dreams to Reality – SME Focus

Learn from yesterday, live for today, hope for tomorrow.
—Albert Einstein

Big organisations we see today are all products of small beginnings. To build a company requires great vision, commitment and passion. It does not cost money for visionaries to dream. Every visionary has that spark in his eyes that allows sleepless nights, dreaming of the many possibilities to come.

In the creation of the vision, there is usually the attempt to answer questions that have to do with our motivating factor for setting up the company or the organisation. We sit down for hours clarifying what we consider is the purpose – a higher calling, compelling, life-changing, innovative and measurable reason why we do what we do.

The following are a few tips to determine your way to success. Write them in stone and act accordingly:

- Anticipate intentionally.
- Value change, competitive edge and advantage, behavioural swings in people and society.
- Be deliberate in your embrace of change and remain religiously teachable.
- Plan what is needed to achieve your dreams: people, resources and environment (the big shifting unknown constant).
- Sell your ideas and believe your dreams.
- Focus on opportunity.
- Avoid distractions and the fear of failure.

Courage and belief in yourself are necessary ingredients to move from dream to reality. The grit and grind of the slow pace, the loneliness of thoughts and the need for speed to market are parts of the basket of focus.

Stay rigorously committed to the singular objective of achieving your dream, which is always in two parts: 1) not dwelling in the past, but 2) reaching ahead to achieve a vision of a prosperous future.

ACTION AND PASSION

Fail early, fail often, but always fail forward.
—John C. Maxwell

Action: Executing your plans; the nowness of action helps to reduce fear and increase courage to forge ahead.

At this point, I will chip in a little personal note I carry around. It contains amongst other things the ANTS lesson:

A: Attitude of initiative. Ants don't need anyone to tell them to get started.

N: Nature of integrity. Ants work faithfully and need no accountability to keep them doing right.

T: Thirsty for industry. Ants work, and will replace their anthill if and when destroyed.

S: Source of insight. Ants store provisions for rainy days.

To conclude, SME go under or crash, especially in challenging times, as a result of several combinations of reasons. In my opinion, two stand out:

1. fear of leadership and
2. working hard on yesterday's dreams.

Fear of change is the most common fear experienced when our world is shaken, as it is presently. We lose our bearings, we feel insecure and we grasp for anything that can bring certainty.

In this desperation for a solution, mistakes and failures set in. We hide failures, we blame everyone and everything, we run from ourselves and even throw in the towel. In the face of challenges, changes and uncertainty, we should accept failures, make amends and adjustments and *go forward!*

I leave you with four quotes from John C. Maxwell in his book, *Leadershift:*[1]

1. 'Continually learn, unlearn, and relearn'.

2. 'See the big picture as the picture keeps getting bigger'.

3. 'Move forward courageously in the midst of uncertainty'.

4. 'Realize today's best will not meet tomorrow's challenges'.

NOTE

1. John C. Maxwell, *Leadershift: 11 Essential Changes Every Leader Must Embrace* (Nashville, TN: HarperCollins Leadership, 2019), 9, 12, 15, 16.

A Third-Party View of the Author, Ifie Sekibo, and the Birth of Heritage Bank

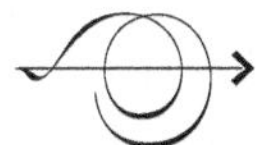

Described variously by his admirers and colleagues as a banking prodigy, a tenacious entrepreneur, passionate game changer and a results-oriented professional with a proven track record in turnaround management, Mr Ifie Sekibo, on assumption of office as the pioneer Managing Director and CEO of Heritage Bank in 2013, came with an enviable track record of successfully turning around several ailing businesses.

Nevertheless, as the managing director of Heritage Bank, Sekibo showed early enough a thorough and profound understanding of an industry with many entrenched players, making it clear to his team that a new operator must, based on the bank's mission, fashion out a unique path to be reckoned with in the market. 'Our vision is simple and clear; today, we might look quite new in the market, but our idea of what this bank should be is clear from day one. We want to be a bank that people will believe and we want to lead in the knowledge that generation banking is the way to go', Sekibo said at the inception of the bank.[1]

With a unique philosophy to 'Create, Preserve and Transfer Wealth' across its teeming customers, and a market share considered insignificant at inception, Ifie Sekibo as Managing Director and CEO promised that Heritage Bank would, in a matter of time, become a force to be reckoned with in the industry. This, he promised, would be accomplished by treating each customer as unique and coming up with financial services designed with a deep understanding of his or her needs and wants.

Walking his talk, Heritage Bank grabbed the attention of the industry and the banking public with the beautiful design of its buildings and interior of its banking halls at its inception. The Bank's branches, referred to as Experience Centres, in their green and white hues, were designed to denote core values, including innovation, tenacity, respect, quality service delivery, among others.

Less than two years into its operations, Heritage Bank, which was originally licensed as a regional bank, signified its intention to join the big league when it bided, alongside other established players in the industry to acquire the defunct Enterprise Bank, which was then being overseen by the Assets Management Corporation of Nigeria (AMCON). Against all expectations, Heritage Bank, under the expert guidance of Sekibo, beat the giants of the industry including Fidelity, Skye, Diamond and others, paying the total sum of N65 billion asking price for the acquisition of Enterprise Bank, within the time frame specified by AMCON.

The acquisition of Enterprise Bank by Heritage Bank was described as the single most significant event in the Nigerian banking sector in 2014. Even more significant is the fact that the acquisition of Enterprise Bank with its network of over 160 branches, over 177 ATMs, 57 Cash Centres and 2000 POS Terminals spread across major markets and commercial centres in the country, transformed Heritage Bank from a regional to a national bank.

'Having secured all relevant regulatory approvals, we are pleased to announce the beginning of a seamless integration of both entities – Heritage Bank and Enterprise Bank, into a bigger and stronger financial institution that is positioned to play a big role in the much envisaged transformation of the nation's financial sector in line with the country's stature as Africa's largest economy', Sekibo told journalists at a media briefing in Lagos late 2014.[2] He had earlier promised to make the bank more successful, create more value and improve on what AMCON had done with Enterprise Bank.

There is no better indication of the resilience with which Sekibo and his team had gone about fulfiling this promise than a look at the audited financial statement announced by Heritage Bank for 2015, which represents its first full operating year since its acquisition of the former Enterprise Bank. The financial statement, released in July, showed that the bank recorded gross earnings of N24.2 billion in the year under review, while its net interest income stood at N12.2 billion, with a profit after tax of N1.1 billion. As a measure of growing confidence among the banking public, Heritage was also able to attract

N312 billion in deposits from customers during the period, while its assets stood at N483.4 billion at of the end of 2015.

'This result is a testimony to the increased acceptability of Heritage Bank's innovative products and services by the banking public. It is also a reward for the diligent commitment of the staff and management of the bank to our mission to create, preserve and transfer wealth across generations', Sekibo said in an interview.[3]

'The positive response to these efforts gives us assurance of improved financial performance in 2016 leading to enhanced returns to our investors', he added while promising that Heritage Bank would reciprocate the patronage of customers and good-will from stakeholders to further introduce new and bespoke services driven by cutting edge technology designed to empower businesses and individuals with opportunities to achieve economic prosperity.

As a measure of confidence in the Bank, in 2018, Heritage was selected by the Central Bank of Nigeria (CBN) as its pilot partner to unveil, administer and manage the N3 billion Youth Innovative Entrepreneurship Development Programme, an initiative aimed at creating sustainable wealth and employment with focus on sectors such as Agricultural Value Chain, Cottage Industry, Mining and Solid Minerals, Creative Industry and Information and Communications Technology.

The selection of Heritage Bank for the programme was no doubt based on the immense success the bank recorded in a similar initiative tagged Young Entrepreneurship Business Training Programme (YEBTP), which it carried out earlier in the year in conjunction with the Centre for Values in Leadership (CVL). Heritage Bank empowered 100 aspiring start-up entrepreneurs under the initiative, which involved grooming, mentoring and financing. Yet, YEBTP is a demonstration of the Bank's commitment to using financial inclusion to boost entrepreneurship development, which is critical to its mission to create, preserve and transfer wealth across generations as defined in its blueprint. This has led the Bank to evolve different initiatives in support of SMEs and micro enterprises with the ultimate aim of helping Nigeria to build a resilient economy. For one, Heritage Bank raised the bar in the area of financial inclusion with its pilot 'Corner Shop' for traders and artisans of the Gbagada plank market, Lagos State, as part of its Agent Banking Scheme.

With the initiative, Heritage Bank Limited has been giving traders at the plank market the opportunity to enjoy financial services without having to go to a bank branch. Then, there is also the Bank's pioneering portable POS solution named 'PortaPOS', which was introduced in 2014. Heritage PortaPOS has several distinct features including the ability to accept all EMV Chip & PIN cards, MasterCard, Verve and Visa cards. It is portable and light. It has a long-lasting and rechargeable Li-Ion battery and it syncs to phone and printer via Bluetooth technology. Heritage Bank's Micro, Small and Medium Enterprises (MSME) Clinic offers holistic advisory services for SMEs in the area of business diagnostics, financial literacy, entrepreneurship development, among others.

Then, there is the innovative Heritage Bank Micro Small and Medium Enterprises Investment Protection Fund – a non-collateralised funding option fortified with insurance to take care of the default risk inherent in the SME scheme. The Fund, designed with the sole aim of enhancing the growth and rejuvenation of the MSME sector, is indicative of the unique approach to SME funding in the country. Under the scheme, Heritage Bank offers such services as idea fine-tuning, advisory, set-up, financials and customised product development as well as other support programmes aimed at developing the survival and growth capabilities of the MSME entrepreneurs. It was through the scheme for instance, that the Bank supported famous musician, Dbanj, in his launching of KOKO AGROPRENEUR. 'We at Heritage Bank are pleased to partner with Dbanj in the "Nagropreneur" (Nigeria Agricultural Entrepreneur) initiative. As a bank whose ideology is to create, preserve and transfer wealth across generations, this initiative falls right within our purview', Bayo Ogunnusi, Group Head of SME Banking, Heritage Bank, said.

Just recently, Heritage Bank launched an exclusive biometric identity card for members of the Performing Musicians Employers' Association of Nigeria (PMAN). PMAN Membership Identification Card (PMBIC) is aimed at driving accessibility, security, trust, convenience and cost effectiveness, which are the defining features of a new partnership blossoming between Heritage Bank and the bourgeoning Nigerian music and entertainment industry. Renewable annually, the PMBIC, according to Heritage Bank, will serve as the official PMAN identification card that qualifies the holder as a genuine member of the association and entitles the artiste to enjoy the myriad of benefits and privileges due to registered members. With the launch of this product, Heritage Bank has consolidated its place as Nigeria's most innovative banking service provider and a pioneer in the biometric card services in the industry.

Mr Ifie Sekibo and his very vibrant team at Heritage Bank have also been busy in the areas of equity and project financing. Acting as sole financier or financial adviser, Heritage Bank has financed projects in various fields, including oil and gas, aviation and haulage as well as the public sector. Key among such projects are the successful financing of Forte Oil Plc's acquisition of 100 brand-new Mercedes Benz product delivery trucks for haulage, logistics and product transportation; and the Project Finance Facility to PIPP LVI GENCO to set up a 6.5 megawatts power generating plant and a 25km distribution network to power public utilities in Lekki, Victoria Island, and Ikoyi, Lagos. Notably, both projects were in 2014 at a time the Bank can be said to be at its infancy. Also, between 2013 and 2014, Heritage Bank midwifed various projects in the entertainment sector valued at over $100 million USD. In October this year, the Bank initiated a N200 million loan facility for young graduates willing to go into small-scale businesses.

The facility, a revolving soft loan, which comes with a financial and management advisory was targeted at National Youth Corps members, who upon passing demonstrate intentions of starting up small scale businesses. The Bank said the idea of the loan became necessary because small businesses constitute the core engine of the economy, stressing that 'with a business, you can bequeath a legacy that will outlive you'.

Apart from its core banking mandate, Heritage Bank has also distinguished itself in the area of Corporate Social Responsibility (CSR). On this score, the bank has donated to Lagos State Security Trust Fund (LSSTF), sponsored the Port Harcourt Amateur Golf Tournament now known as Heritage Cup Golf Tournament and recently sponsored an annual sporting event for secondary schools in Nigeria with the aim of discovering and rewarding talents. The project, known as Skoolympics, is aimed at building a heritage of champions using Lagos State for the pilot scheme and has the African queen of the tracks and two-time Olympic medalist, Mary Onyali-Omagbemi, as the Brand Ambassador. Heritage Bank's CEO, Ifie Sekibo, says the idea behind Skoolympics is the holistic development of young people, fostering their physical, social and emotional health. 'The benefits of Skoolympics reach beyond the impact on physical well-being and the value of the educational benefits of Skoolympics should not be underestimated', Sekibo said while officially flagging off the project in Lagos at a crowded corporate forum presentation.

The strides recorded by Heritage Bank under Ifie Sekibo in its relatively short time of existence have earned the bank commendations from several quarters. To the Chartered Institute of Bankers of Nigeria (CIBN), the foremost professional association of bankers in Nigeria, Heritage Bank's continued deployment of innovative banking services and preference for quality workforce is a strong proof that professionalism still thrives in the Nigerian banking system. 'It is our delight that Heritage Bank is making remarkable impact within the Nation's Banking industry. We recognise and appreciate your sense of innovation as a bank which reflects on the banking services you offer', Otunba (Mrs) Debola Osibogun, the immediate past president/chairman of Council, CIBN, said during the Institute's stakeholder engagement visit to Heritage Bank's corporate head office in Lagos.

Otunba Osibogun, noted that Heritage Bank has brought remarkable freshness to the delivery of banking services in Nigeria. The then CIBN President also congratulated the Bank's Managing Director, Mr Ifie Sekibo, on his investiture as an honorary senior member of the CIBN. 'As a member of the CIBN Governing Council, I have no doubt in your capability to be able to drive Heritage Bank's innovative vision and strategic developmental decision. It is our hope that you will continue to thrive on the professionalism and excellent banking that you have established here', she said. One of the reasons for the visit by the CIBN team was to encourage bankers to sign the new Code of Conduct in the Nigerian Banking Industry, an important strategic initiative that is designed to elevate good banking practices and ethics aimed at restoring public confidence in the banking system. And it was cheering to note that there was an open display of the signed Code of Conduct form by Mr Sekibo, indicating Heritage Bank's commitment to the highest standard of professional ethics in the industry. The Bank achieved another milestone in 2015 when it got the ISO/INEC 27001:2013 certification award in recognition of its commitment to effective and secured financial systems.

Heritage Bank, which set a record as the only bank in Nigeria to get the certification award in less than three years of operation, thereby joining the league of foremost players in the sector, including CBN, which are ISO/INEC 27001 compliant. The award was presented on behalf of the British government to the bank in Lagos on Wednesday, 5th August 2015, by the Deputy High Commissioner of the United Kingdom in Nigeria, Mr Ray Kyles. 'It is not an easy task. This award remains a cornerstone of your reputation', Kyles said while commending Heritage Bank for setting high standards in the financial industry.[4] 'This is a day to beat our chest. Heritage Bank is an idea, not a bank. We are a service company providing banking service; and we are the best in the class of security of our information systems. It means funds kept with us are safe. This award is a validation of our mission to promote high ethical standards, integrity, and good business practices', Sekibo said while receiving the award and further noted that banking is a business of risks management, from assets to data.

The ISO, a product of the British Standard Institute (BSI), is an independent, non-governmental organisation, the whose members are the standard organisations of its 164 member countries. It is the world's largest developer of voluntary international standards and facilitates world trade by providing common standards between nations. 'When we came on board, we were thinking of how to manage ten years of accumulated business. Indeed, in the last one year, we have gathered experiences that no school could teach us because we were the most regulated bank', Sekibo further added.

Such commendations negate recent attempts to de-market Heritage Bank, which has been built into a stallion of resilience by the CEO in the past three years. The good thing is that the industry's regulatory body, CBN, through Isaac Okoroafor, its Director of Corporate Communication, has assured customers of the bank to carry out their transactions as the bank remains one of the best managed banks in the country.

To most banking professionals in the country, the continuing attempt to de-market Heritage Bank is nothing but the handiwork of some powerful persons and their associates who are seemingly opposed to the astronomical growth of the bank. 'The management team at Heritage bank has shown resilience and tenacity. They have shown that they are not the type of bankers that would bend the rules of banking to accommodate unwholesome interests. Heritage bank is not a place where supposed powerful influences can overwhelm or over awe the management team to access huge unsecured loans', a group, Niger Delta Professionals in Banking and Financial Sector (NDPBFS) declared in a recent statement signed on its behalf by National President Joshua Amachre.[5]

True, discerning professionals in the very sensitive banking and financial services sector have been quick to ascribe the success of Heritage Bank to the professionalism and uncommon tenacity of the bank's managing director. Indeed, Mr Ifie Sekibo is clearly tailor-made for the job. An alumnus of the renowned Harvard Business School OPM class (2006-2008) and a Fellow of the Institute of Chartered Accountants of Nigeria (2002), Sekibo is a thoroughbred banker with over two decades of professional work experience spanning across the financial services and energy sectors. He is reputedly a steadfast entrepreneur, passionate game changer and results-oriented professional. These attributes consistently drive his vision to lead vibrant teams to mobilise strategic investments and capital injection to resuscitate and restructure moribund companies to the path of sustained profitability. Mr Sekibo is a valued member and Fellow of a number of professional institutes including: Institute of Directors, Chartered Institute of Bankers of Nigeria, Institute of Credit Management, Institute of Corporate Governance of Nigeria, etc.

NOTES

1. Odunewu Segun, 'Heritage of Banking Success', *National Daily Newspaper*, 5 July 2016, https://nationaldailyng.com/heritage-of-banking-success/, accessed 18 June 2020.

2. Chijioke Nelson, 'Consolidating 2014 Acquisition Drive, Initiatives with Seamless Integration', *The Guardian Business*, 20 January 2015; https://guardian.ng/business-services/money/consolidating-2014-acquisition-drive-initia-tives-with-seamless-integration/, accessed 18 June 2020.

3. 'Nigeria: Heritage Bank Posts N1.5b Profit One Year After Acquiring Enterprise Bank', Footprint to Africa, 7 July 2016, http://footprint2africa.com/featured/nigeria-heritage-bank-posts-n1-5b-profit-one-year-acquiring-enterprise-bank/, accessed 18 June 2020.

4. 'Heritage Bank Bags ISO Award, Sets New Banking Record', Jawonja News, 13 August 2015, https://yemojanewsng.com/heritage-bank-bags-iso-award-sets-new-banking-record/, accessed 18 June 2020

5. Dyepkazah Shibayan, 'Powerful People Desperate to Tarnish Heritage Bank's Image, Say Banking Professionals', *The Cable*, 21 November 2016, https://www.thecable.ng/powerful-people-desperate-tarnish-heritage-banks-image-say-banking-professionals, accessed 18 June 2020.

Publishing Services by
EVANGELISTA MEDIA & CONSULTING

Via Maiella, 1
66020 San Giovanni Teatino (CH) – Italy

publisher@evangelistamedia.com

www.evangelistamedia.com

 /evangelistamediaconsulting

 evangelista_media_consulting

SCAN THE QRCODE BELOW TO CONTACT US: